I WANT TO BE WHERE THE NORMAL PEOPLE ARE

Rachel Bloom

CORONET

First published in Great Britain in 2020 by Coronet
An Hachette UK company

1

Copyright © Handsome Iguana, Inc. 2020

The right of Rachel Bloom to be identified as the Author of the Work has been
asserted by her in accordance with the Copyright, Designs and Patents Act 1988.

Photograph p.iii © Christian Kilrain Carter Coleman

Print book interior design by Abby Reilly.

Unless I say otherwise, all names of my childhood friends, classmates, managers,
and love interests have been changed, as have some identifying details.

A CIP catalogue record for this title is available from the British Library

Hardback ISBN 978 1 529 35463 8
Trade Paperback ISBN 978 1 529 35464 5
eBook ISBN 978 1 529 35465 2

Printed and bound in Great Britain by Clays Ltd, Elcograf S.p.A.

Hodder & Stoughton policy is to use papers that are natural, renewable
and recyclable products and made from wood grown in sustainable
forests. The logging and manufacturing processes are expected to
conform to the environmental regulations of the country of origin.

Hodder & Stoughton Ltd
Carmelite House
50 Victoria Embankment
London EC4Y 0DZ

www.hodder.co.uk

In memory of Adam Schlesinger, who never cared what "normal protocol" was, hence organizing his own photo shoot for a Crazy Ex-Girlfriend *episode in which he posed as a fictional composer named Elliott Ellison, the photo of which would only be shown for less than five seconds.*

NORMAL

What is normal?
Every day we hear it as something everyone should be.
But should they really?
What is the so-called standard that we mold and fit
ourselves through an invisible corset to be accepted in
society all our life?
Is it based on looks?
Humor?
Brains?
Or is it something else, something in your heart that you're
born with, and cannot gain from practice or experience?
If no one is sure what it is, then why are people harshly
judged by its qualifications
every single tedious day?
I rack and rack my brain to figure out what it is.
Who is normal?
Your neighbors?
Your Freddie Prinze Jr. look-alike crush?
Your dog?
What appears to be normal may in fact be the opposite;
a juicy ripe apple with a green worm inside.
My theory is that every apple, whether rotten or ripe on
the outside, has a tiny little green worm inside that's just
dying to crawl out.
And one day, it will.
—Written by Myself, Age Twelve

PART 1:

NORMAL PEOPLE DON'T GET BULLIED

PULL DOWN YOUR PANTS AND LET'S COMPARE TRAUMAS

Were you bullied in middle school? Yeah? You were?

Bullshit.

You weren't bullied. *I* was bullied. I am the ultimate judge of bullying and I conclude that I was bullied and you were not bullied. So says me, court adjourned, gavel goes bang bang.

Most people *say* they were bullied in middle school. But what they're describing isn't bullying; it's just feeling out of place. And hey, that's fair; middle school *is* awkward, even for, per the title of this book, "the normal people." For "the normal people," I gather that middle school was annoying but that the personal conflict never got darker than a story in the Disney's One Saturday Morning animated series *Pepper Ann*. (There's only so much darkness to be mined in the life of a protagonist described by the theme song as "Much too cool for seventh grade.")

3

Over time, I became resentful of these normies / happies / reggies / those too cool for seventh grade who conflated run-of-the-mill middle school awkwardness with "bullying." So in adulthood, I started to call them out on their shit. "Oh, I'm sorry, were you excluded from Sarah's birthday party that one time? Fuck you. I routinely found notes that said 'Ugly' and 'Looser' in my locker. And no, typos don't make the insults hurt less. I warsh they did!"

By my mid-twenties, every middle school story that didn't send someone into therapy later in life became open season for my ridicule. "Aw, you got your period right before you went onstage for the talent show and it was awkward? Well I was so routinely harassed at every talent show that by the time I got to seventh grade, I was grateful the only booing I got was one person shouting, 'Rachel sucks!'"

(Side note: Here's that actual diary entry from 3/26/2000):

"2 days ago I was in the talent show. I got no boos, except for a barely audible 'Rachel sucks!' I did super well."

You may have noted that, in my need to "out-trauma-story" people, I turned into a bully myself. To that I say: Oooooooooh look who's so smaaaaaaaart it's youuuuuuu you're so smaaaaaaaart why don't you have a smaaaaaaaaart party (but please invite me because being left out of parties triggers my insecurity).

As a mature adult, I've come to learn that trauma is real for everyone and just because someone had it worse doesn't mean you didn't have it bad.[*] And I'm the first to admit that my middle school horror stories *paaaaaaale* in comparison with those of many other people. I was never physically attacked, the bullying never resulted in self-harm, and it had nothing to do with my race, sexual orientation, gender identity, or socioeconomic status. I was a "looser," yes, but a white, straight, upper-middle-class, cis-gendered, able-bodied one. Of course, this caveat regarding privilege applies to many other conflicts in my life so feel free to apply this footnote to any of the conflicts throughout the book as you see fit!

However, when I occasionally dip my toe back in the game of middle school trauma one-upmanship, I do have this story: When I was in seventh grade, the popular kids paid the most popular guy in school to ask me out as a prank.

Haha, trauma checkmate, motherfucker!

---

[*] See, Dr. Yakamura? I DO listen in our sessions. Now get off my ass.

The story: In 1999, I was a seventh grader in Manhattan Beach, California, at the creatively named Manhattan Beach Middle School. And I went to school with some real dumbfucks. Dumbfucks with no sense of culture, introspection, or the difference between plural and possessive. I know middle school is famous for being filled with dumbfucks, but there really is a special brand of dumbfuckery unique to the Southern California beach suburbs. We're talking people named "Tiffany" or "Gaskin." Most of their conversations involved wakeboarding and burritos. People who think "melanoma" means a really awesome tan, people who asked me, "So did you guys write that whole thing?" after the drama department put on *Into the Woods*. No, Gaskin. We didn't.

When I was in middle school circa 1999, a lot of movies came out that explored the popular vs. unpopular caste system: *She's All That*, *Never Been Kissed*, et cetera. Most people walked away from these films understanding that the moral was that the bullies were bad. But my bullies were so fucking stupid they thought the heroes of those movies were the BULLIES. The second a new teen flick came out, my bullies would literally adopt the clothing and verbal styles used by the bullies in the films. I guess they loved the characters' cool fashion, their awesome cars, and the biting insults said by the twenty-eight-year-old actors pretending to be sixteen.

One of my dumbfuck bullies even wrote a review for the school paper about my favorite movie, Todd Solondz's *Welcome* *to the Dollhouse.* She called it one of the "funniest comedies" she'd ever seen "because the girl in it is so ugly."[*]

And now we come to me, a real-life Todd Solondz hilarious uggo. I was a pale kid with transition-lensed glasses and a rolling backpack, with lopsided bangs that I, for some reason, cut myself. I was so naturally scrawny that there was a rumor going around that I was anorexic but also a rumor that I wasn't cool enough to be anorexic. I sang show tunes under my breath and used words like "parlance." My favorite outfit: sweatpants, Payless zipper shoes, and an oversize T-shirt that featured Betty Boop dressed as all of the Spice Girls, the caption of which said, appropriately, BOOP WORLD. Basically, my style sensibility was "the best prizes at a Chuck E. Cheese."

I dug myself in my loser hole deeper in every way possible. Being an oversharer, I told a few people of the medical peril of having a mole on my face removed because it might be cancerous, which earned me the nickname "Chemo." I won a grandparent/grandchild look-alike contest at the local mall that was broadcast on the local CBS News. When others were reading *The Baby-Sitters Club*, I was immersed in William Peter Blatty's *The Exorcist*.

Activity time: In eighth-grade English class, bring up the scene in which Regan fucks herself with a crucifix until she

---

[*] Reviewing Todd Solondz's *Happiness*, this same writer called it a "heartwarming will-they-or-won't-they romantic comedy about a grown man going after his crush!"

bleeds! Then draw the look on your teacher's face in the box below!

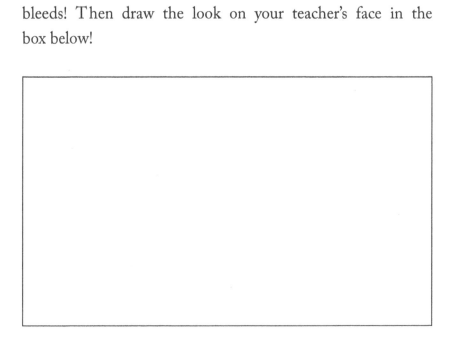

If only I could say that my personality in hindsight was awesome and no one "got me," but this is disproved by the seventy-two DVDs' worth of home movies that my mother gifted me on my thirtieth birthday. Thanks to these DVDs, I have concrete proof my personality was pretty insufferable. When I watch those, I cringe at every word that comes out of my mouth. I am so insecure in my own skin that my speech pattern is a collection of half-baked impressions of the adults that I respect: my mother, my father, Ethel Merman, and Joan Cusack in *Addams Family Values*.

I also wish I could say that I didn't care that I was made fun of; that I let my freak flag fly and was proud of being a weirdo. But I hated who I was. I hated my hair, my voice, my clothes.

It was agonizing because I DESPERATELY wanted to be popular. I wanted to hang with Gaskin and learn to surf and have parents who were retired jocks who worked in real estate. By day, I vocally detested the melanoma'd beautifuls, but by night, I imagined myself as one of them. I never did the math on how I could actually make the transition to being popular because I'm bad at math. It was much easier to imagine snapping my fingers and just being a new person. Sometimes I'd use the two-column format in Microsoft Word to write fake high school newspaper articles about my future self in which I was the homecoming queen, a cheerleader, and dating my longtime crush. (The floppy disk that held this pioneering work in the genre "self-fanfiction" has been sadly lost to time.)

A teensy-tiny fact to add to the mix: This whole time, I was wrestling with a darkness in my mind that I later realized was obsessive-compulsive disorder. I'll go into this later (it's a fun beach read!), but for now let's just say that it was a shadow over my life that colored everything I did. Get excited!

Anyway, I made it my secret mission to impress the popular kids. But of course I was still…me, so my grandest efforts made everything worse. "I'm gonna enter the school lip sync contest and do 'Adelaide's Lament' from *Guys and Dolls*! THAT'LL make them respect me!" I genuinely thought my talent and dedication to my craft would impress them. As I tried harder and harder to make a mark in the only ways I knew how, my desperation made me even more delicious bully meat. With every effort, I could feel myself sweating gallons of bully pheromones that even bullies from neighboring schools could smell from miles away, like I was a house cat in heat and they were the brawny neighborhood strays tearing open my screen door to impregnate me.

Had I not been so desperate to prove myself, I probably could have lived peacefully under the radar. My friend Gillian, for instance, wasn't bullied nearly as much as I was yet was arguably just as weird. She regularly wore tie-dye ponchos and reindeer headbands at Christmastime, plus her parents owned *three* harpsichords. But she got made fun of a lot less because she didn't react to the bullies. She was happy with who she was and genuinely didn't give a shit about what they thought of her. It was badass.

By the time of the BIG PRANK, I had actually started to learn from Gillian and given up on my popularity quest. My last attempt at coolness had been a bust: I spent $80 of allowance money on "Roxy" brand shirts, but it didn't make a dent. Maybe Gillian was right; us losers just needed to live in quiet peace with our weirdness.

Shortly after coming to this conclusion, Gillian and I formed a group of fellow loser friends with whom we'd eat lunch on a sad tuft of grass every day. There's always that one shitty spot in every school that feels as if the architect said, "Hmm, I need to design someplace secluded and moist for the uncool kids." So, I'm eating a turkey sandwich on my loser tuft and along comes this girl Nicola. Background on Nicola: She *was* an upper-tier loser who used to eat lunch with us sometimes but was now working her way up to mid-level wannabe. Mid-level wannabe was about two tiers below true popularity, so she could sit at the popular table but only if she got stabbed and needed a place to wait for the ambulance.

Nicola came up to me and stated, "Rachel. The popular kids wanna talk to you." Oh no. This can't be good. Embracing my new mantra of "stay away from the popular people and blend into the background," I refused to go over there.

But the next day, it was the same thing. Nicola came over, her double A's pushed up to her chin, and said, "Rachel, the popular kids really wanna talk to you." And I again refused. The same thing happened the day after that. It was like some sort of old rabbinic parable about a man and his goats and the moral of the story ends up being "Be grateful for the soup you have."

After I'd ignored Nicola for a full week, two of the popular girls actually followed me as I walked home. They said, "We have something REALLY important to tell you, come with us!" When I refused, they started pulling on my hoodie. Thinking fast, I said, "I can't, I have to go to the hospital, my uncle has cancer!" (Years later, my uncle ended up actually dying of cancer, so I blame you, Brittany and Lauren.)*

---

* A family member in the hospital became my go-to gut reaction whenever I felt in danger. When I lived in New York, I was walking home at 3:00 a.m. one time and I felt like a guy was following me. Without missing a beat, I whipped out my cell phone and went, "What, Mom? Dad's in the hospital! I'll be right there!" and started running. So first of all, even in mortal danger, I felt like I needed an excuse to run away from a man for fear of offending him. But second of all, I assumed he'd take pity on me in that moment. "Well, I can't rape her now, the poor girl's dad's in the hospital. I hope he's okay."

I was getting tired of the whole thing, though, so when Nicola came up to me the next week at lunch and said, "Rachel. The popular kids wanna talk to you," I finally asked, "Why? Why, Nicola?" Nicola said, "Because Devon McElroy wants to ask you out."

Now, obviously, his name was not really Devon McElroy. I've changed his name to protect his privacy. His real name was Ryan Hamilton.

I knew this had to be a joke. I had barely spoken to Devon McElroy. He wasn't even one of my main bullies. He sat on the bully bench and would only sub in when another bully got injured. I truly had no read on Devon/Ryan's personality and, outside of his social status, I was in no way attracted to him. But still, I was intrigued. I mean, I KNEW the whole thing had to be a joke. There is no way that a popular guy wanted to ask me out. At the same time, there was a part of me deep down that thought...maybe my efforts to be cool finally worked. Maybe Devon noticed my Roxy shirts and appreciated my ability to sell the story of a song. Plus, I was growing boobs. I didn't wear a bra yet (which got me teased in the locker room), so maybe Devon had clocked my new nipples curiously poking out from under my shirt like the noses of two precocious mice. Deciding that if Devon really loved me I could learn to love him back, I decided to see what he had to say.

By the time I walked over to where the popular kids sat, word had spread around the entire school that Devon McElroy was going to ask out Rachel Bloom. So as I stood in front of the populars' picnic table, I was also surrounded by about sixty other kids. It felt scary. For the first time in my life, I didn't want all this attention. (That would also be the last time, of course. Winking emoji winking emoji winking emoji.)

"What do you guys want?" I said to them.

"Hey Rachel," croaked Devon McElroy. "I really like you and . . . I was wondering if you'd be my girlfriend."

Seventy-two pubescent eyes (give or take) swiveled toward me. Lost for words, all I could say in that moment was, "Uh . . . okay?"

HUBBUB HUBBUB HUBBUB HUBBUB.

Devon took out a ziplock bag full of Cheetos and said, "Please accept these Cheetos as a token of my affection."

I accepted those Cheetos, everyone cheered, and then, I was launched into a waking dream. For the rest of the day, I was . . . popular. It was just as my self-fanfiction had predicted. I was getting high-fived in the halls, asked to parties, notes were slipped into my locker that said, "U Rool" and for once I didn't mind the spelling error. Two of the popular kids asked me in social studies class how long I thought Devon and I would be together. "Uh . . . until . . . college?" They squeed. Or whatever the late-nineties term for squeeing was. They . . . made a sound like a genie in the bottle being rubbed the right way.

I knew something was wrong when Nicola came up to me after school. Ever since becoming my boyfriend earlier that day, Devon had been notably absent. "Rachel, the popular kids wanna talk to you again." Her voice was solemn. This time, I didn't hesitate to follow Nicola. As I marched with my executioner toward the gallows, I knew that my day in paradise was about to get monsooned on.

Devon was standing in the quad surrounded by various Gaskins. "Hey Devon, what's up?"

"Oh," he said as the Gaskins smirked, "I just remembered that I'm not allowed to have a girlfriend until I'm fifteen. So, uh, yeah, we have to break up."

I could have just run away at that point. But for the first time in my life, I cared about my dignity. So I said, "Oh, that's okay, but I hope we can still be friends." I gave him a hug. And when I left that hug and turned around, they all started laughing. And that's when I knew what I'd known deep down from the beginning. It was a joke. Of course it was.

I walked home in a daze. I'd always been bullied, but this took it to a whole other level of public humiliation. This was a concerted plan to shame me. It took effort, time, and critical thinking skills on the part of my bullies. There was no coming back from this. I felt the dazed numbness of someone newly pariah-ed. The thing I dreaded more than going to school the next day was what my mother might say if she found out about the prank. Shocker time: My parents weren't popular kids, either.* As a result, my mother was particularly sensitive to me

---

* Let's just say the perfect haunted house for the Bloom family would be a single room with a PE teacher in it.

being bullied, her own childhood trauma rising to the surface every time I came home crying from school. I was in enough pain; I didn't want my mother to be as well.

I walked in the door just as my former friend Jackie was leaving a message on our machine. (I'd been close with Jackie in kindergarten but she'd left me around second grade to become an upper-level wannabe.) "Hey Rachel, it's me Jackie, I just wanna say that I heard what the popular kids did. It was a whole thing where they each paid Devon twenty bucks and I think it's so mean and—" Before my mother could come out of the bathroom I picked up the phone. I told Jackie it was fine, all good, I was as cool as a cucumber, as calm as Austin Powers in his swinging sixties shag pad, baby! I hastily hung up on Jackie and deleted the recorded part of the message before my mother could hear anything.

Since I didn't tell my parents what happened, I had no excuse not to go to school the next day. I couldn't complain that I felt "vaguely sick"—I was only allowed to miss school under the most dire of circumstances. So I threw on a Roxy shirt and prayed for anonymity. Maybe everyone forgot the whole thing already?

Of course, people didn't forget. But it wasn't in the way I dreaded.

See, what the popular kids had done was *too* mean. Their scheme was literally a plot out of a shitty teen movie, and even seventh graders could see it was fucked up. I wasn't getting laughed at in the hallway—I was getting apologies. People were coming up to me and saying they were on my side, that they'd never liked those kids anyway, that my "Adelaide's Lament" lip sync was actually pretty sick. At one point, the two girls who grabbed my hoodie / killed my uncle came up to me in tears and begged me not to tell the principal what happened because Devon was their friend and they didn't want him to get suspended. By the end of the day, the whole prank was more of a stain on them than on me. And by the time we got to high school, their stars had faded and they blended into the background where they could never hurt anyone ever again.

Hmm. I realize that this story kind of ends happily. That's a bit too early to happen in this book. *Note to self: Come back to this section later to give it a sadder ending.*

SOME UNORTHODOX WAYS TO DEAL WITH BULLIES

Let's face it: If you're a person of substance, you are going to get bullied in school. But instead of telling yourself that the bullies are "just jealous" (they're not) or trying to learn revenge telekinesis in time for the big dance (you won't, I've tried, it's hard), here are some more out-of-the-box ways to deal with bullying:

LEGAL NOTICE: None of these methods have been tested in any way and I do not hold Rachel Bloom legally responsible for any repercussions in attempting any of these methods. I promise to sign and date on the below line before reading any further.

Signed: _____

Date: _____

And while we're signing stuff, might as well practice your autograph for when you get famous:

_____

Ugh, that last autograph sucked. Do it over:

_____

Method #1: Get rid of the bully's need to bully.

1. Learn to forge your bully's signature. Then, when the school year starts, sign your bully up for as many after-school activities as you can. This also may require setting up a fake email address if the sign-ups are online only—be sure to give your bully something authentic like "caligurl456," not something that shows your hand like judgeycooze@hotmail.com.

2. After you sign your bully up for the school activities, create another fake email address for the teacher at your school in charge of the after-school activities. From this fake email address, email the bully's parents the following:

Hello (INSERT BULLY'S MOM'S NAME HERE)*! Your child has signed up for the following extracurricular activities:*

(INSERT ABSURDLY LONG LIST OF AP-PLICABLE AFTER-SCHOOL ACTIVITIES HERE)

Please note: As your child took up a valuable spot in each activity by signing up before the other students, each missed day of each activity will incur a fee of (INSERT FEE AMOUNT HERE. IF YOU GO TO A PUBLIC SCHOOL, $5; IF YOU GO TO A PRIVATE SCHOOL, $20; IF YOU GO TO A PRIVATE SCHOOL IN LA OR NY, $1,000.) *Thank you!*

Upon reading this email, the bully's parents will be FURI-OUS that the bully signed up for something with cancellation fees without asking, and scream that God, your bully is SO SELFISH and this is SO LIKE THEM. No matter how much the bully protests that they had nothing to do with this, the parent will make them go to every one of these activities. Otherwise, no Lana Del Rey concert, Gaskin!

3. By week two, your bully will be so exhausted from the constant after-school activities, they won't have the energy to bully you. When they're not falling asleep in class because they were up late

finishing homework, they'll be away from school a lot between soccer / debate / golf / dance / Habitat for Humanity / Young Socialists. Hell, they'll even have to miss that precious Lana Del Rey concert to prepare an argument for mock trial the next day.

4. Eventually, your bully will suffer a nervous breakdown. This will be another tragic example of how we're putting way too much pressure on kids these days. But it's awesome for you! Your bully will drop out of school for six months to go to a farm in Oregon where he/she will nurse baby goats back to health and learn the value of living in the present. By the time the bully comes back to school, they will have learned mindfulness and that to bully someone else would be to bully oneself because we are all connected.

5. And that's when YOU swoop in and kick them in the shins! Ha! Stupid Zen baby goat lover!

Method #2: Play into the bully's hero complex.

1. Even the meanest bully thinks that they're the hero of their story. Unless your bully is a true psychopath, every human on earth wants to believe that they are fundamentally good at

heart. So write each of your bullies the following note:

Hey (INSERT BULLY'S NAME HERE),

I know we don't talk that much, but I just wanted to thank you for being the one person at this school who gets me. Even though everyone else makes fun of me, I can tell that you're different. The compassion you show me is sometimes the only thing that gets me through the day. I've been going through a really hard time lately—my dog died of Lyme disease and my aunt was murdered—so any little bit of kindness helps. No wonder you're the most popular kid at school! And btw eff the haters who say that (BULLY'S BEST FRIEND WITH WHOM THEY HAVE A SECRET RIVALRY) *is! Anyway, I'd appreciate you keeping this letter between us because I know only a nice person like you will understand what I'm going through.*

2. This letter serves a few purposes: First and foremost, it isolates the bully from their group, making them feel above everyone else with a holier-than-thou benevolence. Second, it pits the bully against their bullying partner by taking advantage of their subtextual rivalry. There's a tiny risk in sending this letter to multiple bullies, but that's why the last part is important; they won't

share the letter with the other bullies in order to maintain the delusion that they're "special." If you're worried about the letter being too far from the truth, don't worry—upon reading it the bully will retrofit their memories to fit this narrative. Human memory is like some broken computer software that YOU, my friend, can hack!

3. Your bullies will start being nice to you. Now all you have to deal with is compassionate looks from them in the hallway and a condolence call from their moms saying that they hope the police find your aunt's killer soon.

Method #3: Make the parents happy.

In most cases, a bully's anger stems from an unhappy home life. So it stands to reason that if the bully's parents are happy, that means the bully will be happy.

1. Save up all your allowance money to buy the bully's parents / legal guardians a spa gift certificate. Mail the spa gift certificate to them inside an envelope stamped with the school's official seal with a note enclosed saying that the spa certificate is an award from the school given monthly to the parents who have "the best child." The bully's parents will be

proud of the bully, feel good about their parenting skills, and come back refreshed and super in love again from the spa weekend.

2. If your bully's parents are divorced, it gets a little more complicated. Sure, you could save up your allowance money to buy two spa gift certificates, but this won't alleviate the ultimate problem that the bully comes from a broken home. No, I'm afraid that the only real solution is to pull a "Parent Trap" and get your bully's parents back together. It won't be easy, it will take months of your life, and it probably won't work. Nevertheless, it's worth a try. So stop reading this book and get cracking on re-creating your bully's parents' first date!

Method #4: Stop cyberbullying in its tracks.

Thank God social media wasn't a thing when I was in middle school back in 1999. I shudder to think of all the Lois Lowry book review videos I would have Snapchatted while using a Mini-Me face filter. But social media is a reality now, and as you're aware it's one of the main tools used by bullies. To combat this head-on, the only real fix is to completely get off social media. But don't worry: Getting rid of social media isn't uncool; it's called "going on a cleanse." We're gonna take a beat from trying to change the bully and, instead, go internal. It's time to change *yourself*.

1. Before going on the social media cleanse, be sure to post nonstop for a week on social media about how you're going on a cleanse. Use cool phrases like, "This country is just so polarized."

2. The day you close out all of your accounts, come to school wearing a Kabbalah bracelet. Let everyone know you're living in the present, that is, are better than everyone else. Wear only clothes meant to be worn in a yoga class. Find T-shirts with positive affirmations on them—the more nonsensical the better. BREATHE TRUTH is good, DO HUMBLY is great, but #TASTETHEAIR is best.

3. If someone insists on bullying you based on something that has happened on social media without your knowledge, calmly ask them what their meditation mantra is. If they say they don't HAVE a mantra, just give them prayer hands and a pity face. If they tell you a mantra, call them out for being a liar because anyone who DOES meditate knows that your mantra is secret and can't be shared with anyone.

4. And just when they're really confused, that's when YOU kick them in the shins and livestream the video on Instagram!

Method #5: Ruin the bully psychologically (for emergencies only).

1. Look a female bully dead in the eyes and say, "Your pussy stinks like garbage. Everyone can smell your garbage pussy all the time. Your friends will say that I'm lying, that I'm crazy, but they know it's true."

2. This singular moment will ruin your bully's self-confidence for the rest of her life because every woman worries at some point that her pussy stinks like garbage. As your bully grows up, she will be unable to trust anyone, convinced, deep down, that no one is telling her the truth about her garbage pussy. This will especially affect her romantic relationships and hinder her ability to climax.

3. When you run into her years later and she compulsively brings up the moment you called her pussy garbage, say to her, "Oh THAT? I was only kidding that time!" She will go mad with regret at all of the ruined sexual experiences and friendships that came from this complex.

4. For good measure, kick her in the shins.

AND FINALLY, A VERY IMPORTANT NEWSPAPER ARTICLE

(**Printed without permission** from the editorials/ opinions section of my middle school student newspaper, *The Surf Report*. Yes, that's the actual name of the newspaper.[*])

September 27, 2000

Inside Jokes
Can Leave Many Outside
By Rachel Bloom

        Lately around campus, have you heard students saying the weirdest things, and then laughing hysterically over them? Then, when you ask them what they're laughing at, they state in a ditzy tone, "It's an inside joke." Ah yes. The infamous inside joke that

---

[*]   In the same issue, Devon wrote a review of Ruth's Chris Steak House. I haven't attached it here for legal reasons but he gets the restaurant's name wrong, makes up an origin story for it that, according to my research, straight up isn't true and also his review sucks.

people are spewing about lately. To the people in on these, they're funny. To the people not in on the joke, they don't make any sense.

These are usually inspired by an especially funny or weird scenario in which the people involved reminisce about so frequently, that even a phrase sparks the memory. "Inside jokes" unite friends, and can be used in situations of boredom or sadness. But there is a dark cloud to this silver lining.

Sometimes these jokes make people feel left out, and not "in on the secret." They can arouse hurt feelings, and sometimes even invisibly hinder friend-ships. If you have an inside joke with a few friends, but not with another, try to include everyone, or just don't discuss it. Otherwise, you might get some hurt or curi-ous stares peering your way, and some people might even annoyingly bully you to hear the juicy details. But, no matter how annoying or fun "inside jokes" may seem, they're an unavoidable part of our teen culture.

The next time you hear people recognizably laughing over a stupid matter, just roll your eyes and go with the flow because, well, it's an inside joke.

PART 2:

NORMAL PEOPLE WERE NORMAL CHILDREN

FIFTY SHADES OF BROWN / BROWN IS THE WARMEST COLOR / BROWN SUBMARINE

Normal people don't remember the first time they shit in the toilet. I think it's because they aren't in touch with their inner child as much as I am. They see "childhood" as a time in their lives separate from the now, a time lived by the "child version" of themselves. This "child version" is an *Other*: a sticky-fingered, Darkwing Duck–loving Neanderthal. I don't relate to this. I remember being a child very well. I don't see Child Me as an Other. I see her as a very logical start to the conclusion that is current me. So that is why I vividly remember the first time I shit in the toilet.

Or maybe I remember the first time I shit in the toilet because I was four years old when it happened and the entire thing is on videotape.

But even if I weren't four years old when that happened and it wasn't filmed as comprehensively as the Eichmann trial,

I think I'd still remember the moment of shitting in the toilet because it's one of the turning points of my life.

A QUICK ASIDE TO LIST THE TURNING POINTS OF MY LIFE IN ORDER OF APPEARANCE:

- Shitting in toilet
- Barbies suddenly not as compelling to play with, first existential crisis ensues
- Trying for an hour to put in a tampon the day I get my period for the first time because I want to be like my mom
- While riding Disneyland's Haunted Mansion realize that I, too, will die someday; second existential crisis ensues
- 9/11
- First French kiss
- Successfully put in a tampon
- Finally GET *Monty Python and the Holy Grail*
- Lose virginity
- Grandma dies
- Give up on trying to read *The Things They Carried*
- Ears pierced
- Have butt sex
- Married
- Find out in the *Crazy Ex-Girlfriend* writers' room that other people regularly pee in the shower, start peeing in the shower, life changed

I'm probably skipping over some important parts. But let's go back to the fact that I didn't shit in the toilet until I was four years old because I can sense you want to know what the fuck happened.

I'll start out by saying that, by the time I was four years old, I did go *pee* in the toilet. I mean I wasn't insane. The toilet could have all of my pee it liked. But my poop, no. Pooping was my sacred time.

When I felt a number two coming around the corner, I would engage in the same calming, meditative ritual: clearly state to my parents that I needed a diaper now please, put on the diaper, then hole myself up in my room to walk around and pontificate while shitting in that diaper. Diaper Time was a time to dream, to imagine, to free-associate. The release of my bowels released my brain and I credit it as the root of my creativity.

Then, one terrible night in 1991, everything changed. The LA riots had not yet happened, but there was currently an LA riot going on in my stomach. That night I had to poop, but rather than fetch me a diaper on command like usual, my parents decided enough was enough and threw away my diapers. It was now or never. It was toilet time. They were fed up with cleaning the asshole of a person who knew the name of the vice president and fed up with their own fear that I would go to college still in diapers. (No one had told me that being an "Adult Baby" is a fetish lifestyle. Had I known that, my life might be very different now.)

It didn't register with me that I pooped in the toilet super late until I was in high school. I think I casually said at a party, "Eh, I wasn't potty-trained until I was four," and, as the heads of the party guests turned to look at me, I said in what felt like slow motion, "Iiiiiis thaaaaaat weeeeeeeeeeeird?"

So I don't blame my parents for their late-night tough love in 1991. There was also a light at the end of the tunnel; in their efforts to get me to poop in the toilet over the past few months, they had resorted to bribery. "If you poop in the toilet, we'll give you a Hershey's Kiss." "If you poop in the toilet, we'll get you that toy plastic car that you can drive."

Most children would have taken these toy offers and just dropped a deuce into the crapper already. But I was an only child, and a real spoiled fucker of one at that. I knew I could wring more out of these people. So I began to intimidate them, mafia-don-style.

"You come to me on the day of my Barbie's imaginary wedding asking me for a favor. You want me to poop in the toilet and, in exchange, you offer me a toy car. But you do not think to offer the toy gas station that comes with it? How do you suppose I get around in a plastic car with no imaginary gas?"

My parents got on their knees. "Okay, fine, the toy gas station, we'll get you the toy gas station, just please, poop in the toilet." That went on for a while until they finally drew the line at the toy 7/11. I left a poop under the covers of their bed just to send a message.

Suffice to say, by the time that fateful night in 1991 rolled around, I had a pretty sweet cache of loot waiting for me. I was feeling pretty smarmy until the moment came in which I had to actually earn the toys. I went from being that manipulative mafia don to a sniveling child clutching her ass cheeks together, desperate to keep her poopy in. I was afraid of the toilet and its giant hole in the middle that led to the unknown. Toilet equaled void.

I think if I'd kept my parents waiting for a little shorter of a time, until I was, say, three and a half, they might not have videotaped the whole thing. But because I'd waited so long, the only way to cope with the situation was to laugh and capture the whole thing for posterity.

The video opens with me tearfully holding my crotch while standing in our kitchen wearing an oversize T-shirt decorated with the logo of my dad's company. I am pleading with my mother to get me a diaper, and she says in a measured voice, "We threw the diapers away. You have to go in the toilet now."

There's a few more minutes of tearful pleading, me saying I'll never get on the toilet for as long as I live, and then, SMASH CUT TO ME ON THE TOILET! Great edit, Mom. At this point, I am on the toilet, but not pooping yet. I know my parents have won, I know the fateful moment is near, but I can't admit defeat. Because, despite all the toys waiting for me on the other side, I know that this moment will be not only humiliating but a true end of my innocence. Gone will be the days of walking around while shitting myself and arguing with my imaginary friends. Now I will have to sit on this hard chair like all the adults do. I am about to literally flush my childhood down the toilet.

Don't feel too sorry for me that the whole thing is on videotape, by the way. In a bizarre moment, my mother sympathetically asks, "Do you want me to turn off the camera?" And I say, through my tears, "No, keep going."

Finally, I cave, and the moment arrives. My eyes are filled with relief as the poop exits my body. It's hard and big and I remember that it hurt because I'd been holding it in for so long. If you watch the video real close, you will see the eyes of a child who's feeling relief but also seeing her worst fears become true. For as a bit of my childhood is forcibly taken away from me, I do indeed face the void, which I then realize is the inescapability of mortality. For the toilet is the timpani in the funeral march of change, giving us a rhythm as we all march toward the grave.

But you know what? I was wrong that night. Pooping in the toilet wasn't the end of my childhood, and it certainly wasn't the end of me associating bathroom release with creativity. When I poop into the toilet now, I still dream and imagine and free-associate as much as I did when I could spray my brown gift into a Pampers. I love the bathroom, I love the toilet, and I spend a lot of time there. In fact, I'm writing this on the toilet right now. And that, kids, is how you get hemorrhoids.

WHEN I THINK ABOUT LITERALLY ANYTHING, I TOUCH MYSELF

From a young age, I was always sex-obsessed. But not in your typical sitting-on-a-bike-seat thinking "Huh, what is this nice feeling" prepubescent way. My sex obsession was more...sophisticated.

To prove my point, I now present to you some erotic poetry I wrote at age twelve.[*]

NOTE: IF MY PARENTS ARE READING THIS RIGHT NOW, PLEASE STOP AND PROCEED TO THE NEXT CHAPTER. OH GOD, PLEASE DON'T READ THIS.

---

[*]   This erotic poetry was actually the inspiration for my 2012 music video, "You Can Touch My Boobies."

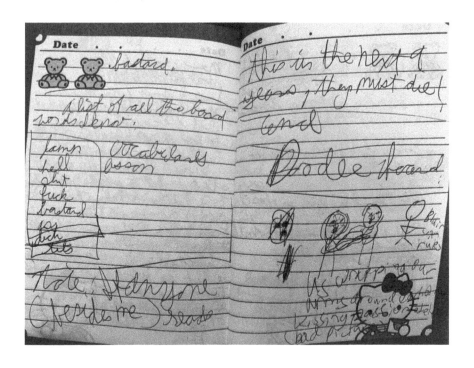

I begin this scintillating diary entry with listing all of the naughty words I know. It's labeled as "vocabulary lesson."

Bad words I know:
Damn
Hell
Shit
Fuck
Bastard
Ass

Dick
Tits

Then, a warning:

NOTE: If anyone (besides me) reads this in the next 9 years, they must die!

Don't worry, it's been longer than nine years, you're safe.

Then, before the poetry starts, I make an attempt at erotic art with the label *DOODLE BOARD*. Those two figures that seem to be hugging far apart like they're at a Catholic school dance? That's my artistic interpretation of sex. To throw the reader further off the scent, a caption at the bottom of the page reads: *(BAD PICTURE)*.

And as a non sequitur, there is a stick-figure doodle with the caption next to it:

Blair Witch Rules. (Because it fucking duz.)

And then, the poetry begins.

Us wrapping our
Arms around each other
Kissing passionately
(next page)

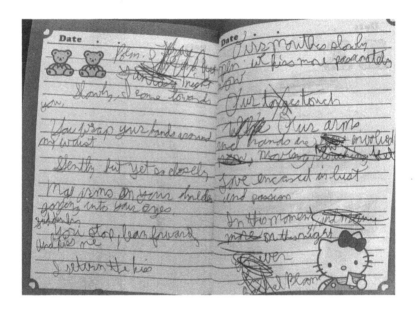

Slowly, I come towards you.

You wrap your hands around my waist

Silently but yet so closely

My arms on your shoulders

Gazing into your eyes

Suddenly

You stop, bend forward

And kiss me

I return the kiss

Our mouths slowly open

We kiss passionately now

~~*Our tongues touch*~~ (I guess this was too X-rated)

Our arms

And hands are involved

Love encased in lust
And passion
In this moment
~~And many more~~ (Redundant, I agree with this cut)
On this night
~~Forever~~
~~By Rachel Bloom~~ (Sexy pen name TBA)

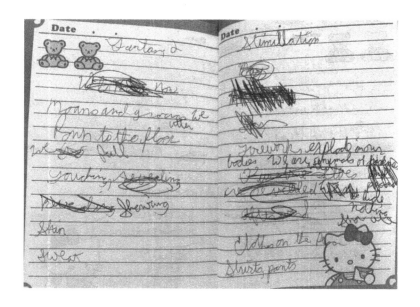

Then there's another poem. Or at least, something that resembles another poem labeled:

FANTASY 2

Moans and groans we utter
Down to the floor

We fall
Touching
Showing
Skin
Sweat
Stimulation
Fireworks explode in our
Bodies
We are animals of
(REDACTED???)
We hide nothing, show all
Clothes on the floor
Shirts
Pants

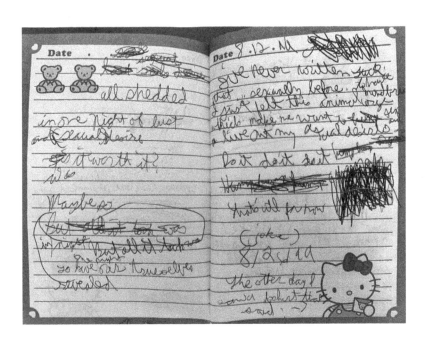

All shedded
In one night of lust
And sexual desire
Was it worth it?
Maybe so
But all it took was
One night
To have our true selves
Revealed

Then I took some time to fan myself off before beginning the next diary entry (which, assumedly, was still the same day).

8-12-99
I've never written that…sexually before. I just felt the animal urge which makes me want sex and to live out my sexual desires.

Then, overcome with the eroticism of my own prose, I go back into poetry mode for one second:

Do it Do it Do it

Then back to normal writing.

That's all for now.

And then, embarrassed by the whole thing and mortified that I put my sexual self on paper for the world to see, I buy the entire thing back with:

(JOKE)

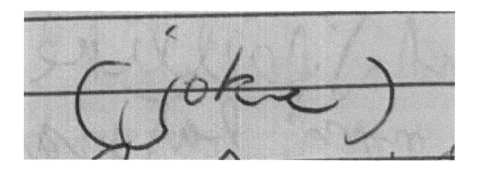

OKAY, NOW I'LL TALK ABOUT THE OCD THING

To be honest, I'm not even 100 percent sure what I had from ages nine to thirteen was "OCD." It's an after-the-fact diagnosis pulled out of my reluctant psychiatrist like a rotten tooth. He prefers more to focus on "the present" and "practical tools I can use day-to-day" rather than on giving me specific diagnoses for things twenty years after the fact. Asshole. But when I do say to him, "Okay, if you HAD to give what I went through a diagnosis, gun to your head…it was OCD, right?" he acquiesces. "Yes, because that falls under a general umbrella of anxiety disorders, which you—" WOO HOO! OCD! FIST PUMP!

I don't WANT to have had OCD. What I want is to know that I wasn't alone. When you're going through your first bout with a mental health issue and don't know any better, the aloneness is the worst part. The feeling that what you have is undefinable, solitary, and it inevitably brings up the question:

If I'm alone in this, what if I'm doing it to myself and does that mean I could stop if I really wanted to? Aloneness = weakness.

But being able to say you have an *illness*? What a beautiful word. Everyone understands *illness*. An *illness* tells me what I'm going through is so common that greater minds than mine have given it a name. A name that labels what it is like chair, table, Steven. If what I have is a labeled *illness*, then I'm not alone.

As magical as labels are, however, they do a shit job at describing how mental *illness* actually feels. Depression, for instance, doesn't feel like this sterile hospital waiting room word: *depression*. It feels like my insides are turning gray, which makes the trees turn gray, which makes all life turn gray, which is the color we all turn eventually because everything leads to nothingness. Hold up, did I just invent postmodernism?!

Just like depression doesn't feel like *depression*, what developed in my mind in childhood didn't feel like *OCD*. If I had to make up my own diagnosis name based on what I felt back then, I would call it "The Bad." Other potential diagnosis names: The Guilty Itch, The Hungry Hungry Manson Caterpillar, Stanley Kubrick's Interpretation of a Mobius Strip, Stomach Ursula, Mr. Bad Shadow Bin Laden, or Oh-God-I-Have-to-Puke-but-the-Puke-Is-My-Thoughts.

The Hungry Hungry Manson Caterpillar found me the summer before fourth grade. I had just been in a really bad bike accident, which may or may not be related. Sometimes my psychiatrist surmises that I may have had head trauma that led to this sudden shift in my brain but then he goes, "Eh, but probably not, never mind."[*] My diagnosis for that is "medical blue balls." A more likely speculation on both our ends is that this shift in my thinking was related to the onset of puberty and all its chemical changes. Or maybe Mercury was in retrograde. At least, that's what everyone in Los Angeles blames their problems on. Whatever the case, I remember when The Bad started. And just like an earlier story, it all starts with being on the toilet.

I was nine years old, taking a dump, when suddenly, a thought popped into my head: I wonder what poo tastes like. You know those weird thoughts that kids have. It's why they touch hot stoves, ask where babies come from, and say precocious things like, "If Daddy's never coming home, does that mean I can have all the beer he left in the fridge?" You know, curiosity for curiosity's sake.

I began to wipe. Then I looked down at the wad of toilet paper in my hand, and then I impulsively put my finger on it. I don't even know if I even touched a part of the toilet paper with poop on it.

Regardless, I put my finger in my mouth. And then

---

[*] Also, I got in the bike accident right near the home of then LA Lakers assistant coach Kurt Rambis. He heard me screaming, ran over, and carried my little bloody body back to my parents' house. Cradled in his seven-foot wingspan, I said, "Are you Kurt Rambis?" I didn't know much about sports but I knew enough to know that Kurt Rambis lived near me. He said yes. Then I said, "Is this a dream?" He said it wasn't. Thanks for saving my life, Mr. Basketball Man.

immediately I ran over to the sink and rinsed out my mouth. And as I did that, I was overcome with something I'd never felt before.

SHAME.

I had never really felt the exotic thing called "shame" before, but I knew the symptoms. I was told that shame made you feel embarrassed and regretful and that you wished you could take something back. It always sounded strange to me, especially because adults told me it was something I should have more of.

(Quick story about my lack of shame in childhood that's too big for a footnote: In first grade, I made up a game on the playground, and when no one was listening to me while I explained the rules, I said defiantly, "If you guys don't listen to me, I'm gonna pull my pants down!" I don't know how I came up with that ultimatum. To show that I meant business, I hitched down the waistband of my culottes a couple inches. Then my culottes fell down. I scrambled to pull them back up and someone shouted, "I can see her ass!" Rather than admit to myself I engineered my own downfall, I immediately came to the conclusion that someone must have run up behind me and pulled down my pants. I told my teacher, who told the principal, which started a grade-wide witch hunt to find "Who pulled down Rachel Bloom's pants??" At the end of that week, my teacher took me in a room. "Rachel, after talking to all the other kids, we've deduced that you pulled down your own pants. Does that make sense?" I nodded.

"Now, with all of the trouble the principal went to this week, plus the fact that you've lied just a bit... don't you think that deserves a star off?" FYI: The "star" system was this teacher's version of low-consequence discipline. Everyone started the year with four gold stars and, if you were bad, you'd get a star off. I currently still had all four stars. When I didn't answer, she repeated the question: "Don't you think you deserve a star off?" I looked her in the face and said, "No. I don't." No. Fucking. Shame.)

So, up until the poop incident, I hadn't felt much shame in my life. But as I symbolically scrubbed my tongue like a low-stakes Lady Macbeth, I was suddenly very sorry. But like, not sorry in the way your parents tell you to say you're sorry. Genuinely, ashamedly, deeply sorry.

I flushed the toilet and rejected this new shameful feeling. I don't like this, I'm not gonna think about this ever again. But then I couldn't stop thinking about it. The rest of the day, the guilt over potentially tasting my poo consumed me. That day turned into a week, which turned into two weeks. I couldn't stop the train of my shameful thoughts. I spent hours reliving that moment, wondering over and over: Why did I do that?

The night before fourth grade started, I was getting desperate. My thoughts of my poo tryst had me in such agony that my stomach hurt. I thought about the other times in the past that I'd done something wrong. Innocent things, like spilling milk or having a tantrum or pulling my own pants down. With all of these innocent transgressions, the thing that always washed it away was coming clean with my parents and apologizing to them.

So that night at dinner, I tried to casually slip this incident into the conversation like a bad stand-up segue.

"Hey, here's something funny...the other day, I tasted my poop. Isn't that funny?"

I heard my parents' forks drop. They stared at me. After ten seconds, my dad said, "What the fuck are you talking about?"

I frantically equivocated with "Well, I don't actually think I tasted it, it was this weird thought I had in the moment, anyway, just wanted to mention it, I thought it was funny."

My parents looked at me, truly grossed out, and a cold river of relief spread through my veins. There. I told them. It was done. As they both calmly lectured me on basic human hygiene, I nodded, trying not to smile. After days of feeling The Guilty Itch, I was finally free.

I settled into bed that night, excited to start fourth grade. I had trouble getting to sleep, which was a normal thing for any kid the night before the first day of school. The usual questions flooded my brain. What should I wear? How would this year be different? What other bad things have I done in my life that I should confess to my parents?

WHOA. That was weird. No, shush. We're done with the whole guilt and confession thing.

Anyway. What will my new teacher be like? What songs will we learn in music class? Remember how my friends and I used to take off our shirts and pretend to be "having sex"? Does that make me a lesbian? Should I tell my parents about that?

And as I thought of everything else in my life for which I should be feeling shame, that was the first night of my life I didn't sleep at all. I. Never. Went. To. Sleep.

As I smiled for my school picture the next day, you'd have never guessed I was a wreck.

Picture of a kid who is definitely okay!

Now, instead of one shameful thing to think about over the next few weeks, I had, like, five. This time, though, I had a game plan. I had learned from the last time that all I had to do was confess each and every one of these things to my parents. I wouldn't confess all the things at once, of course. I didn't want to overwhelm them.

I approached this confession-a-palooza like a slow rollout of a new fashion line. A skirt here, a sweater there. I don't know how fashion works. Basically, once every two days, I'd "casually" tell my parents a thing I was ashamed about. I told them about my friends and me taking off our shirts, I told them that sometimes I pretended the stuffed crayon that I slept with was my boyfriend and so I'd hump it; I think I even retold them about the poop thing just to cover my bases.

Every time I confessed a bad thing, I'd feel the same moment of relief. But then, anywhere from ten minutes to an hour later, the next confession-worthy item would take its place. And this didn't go away when I finished off my list of things. When I finished off that list, a new guilty thought came in. When I purged that thought, a new thought came in after that. And et cetera et cetera. I was being followed by a humpy, poop-covered infinity sign.

I didn't know what was happening to me. After all, we weren't Catholic. I wasn't raised to confess my sins. It just didn't make sense.

One night in the midst of all this going on, I remember watching a *20/20* or *Dateline* special with my parents about kids with obsessive-compulsive disorder. The kids in question were obsessed with things like cleanliness and fire safety. One would wash her hands fifteen times an hour; another would get up repeatedly in the middle of the night to make sure the stove was off. I felt a distant kinship with these kids, but at no point did anyone mention that OCD didn't have to be about cleanliness or safety, so I couldn't relate it to my situation. No one said that OCD meant a pattern of intrusive thoughts (obsessions) and actions to try to calm them (compulsions).

My parents were at just as much of a loss as I was. They'd never heard of this kind of behavior happening with a kid. When it started, I think they just thought I was being…weird? They tried to brush my confessions off. They said they didn't need to hear all these things anymore, that these were my private thoughts, I'd done nothing wrong. So I tried to hold the thoughts in and, when I did that, I began to get crippling stomachaches that accompanied those thoughts. I started missing class a lot to be in the nurse's office. I have a memory of lying there clutching my stomach, the nurse taking pity on me for what she thought was some sort of bug as my mind was overcome with guilt, guilt, guilt. My parents assumed I had some sort of gastrointestinal problem, so they took me to the doctor who did an X-ray. Lo and behold, there was a lot of shit backed up in my stomach. The doctor assumed I just needed more fiber in my diet, so he started me on a daily regimen of a Fiber One breakfast in the morning and a tablespoon of mineral oil at night. But of course that didn't help, either.

At this point, I was already midway through fourth grade. Since I was so uncomfortable in my own skin, I resolved to be as comfortable on the outside as possible. I was never an A-plus dresser, but in the past, this had meant I wore bright, mismatched colors and hilarious T-shirts. Now, though, I opted for baggy sweatpants, plain sneakers, and ridiculously oversize T-shirts that were less hilarious. At the same time, my personal care went out the window. As puberty took hold, my lips got chapped and my skin got dry and I did nothing to rectify the situation. There was too much going on in my mind; I didn't have time to focus on the outside of me. I can only imagine what I must have seemed like to my peers and teachers at this point. I remember working hard to mask the obsessive thoughts from everyone at school. I also remember seeing *Rent* at the Pantages around this time, and the anger in that piece really resonated with me.[*]

When the confessions didn't stop, my parents must have concluded that this was something more than a "weird phase," because they sent me to a therapist. They could tell that I was constantly miserable. At this point, I was eager for help. Please, Mr. Mind Doctor: Fix me.

But the second I sat down in the therapist's office and he asked me what was wrong, I froze. As much as I'd confessed to my parents all of my "sins," I had never confessed what was arguably the most shameful thing: that if I didn't confess these things, I was overcome with terror and stomachaches. I

---

[*] This production starred the one and only Neil Patrick Harris who, years later, would mock my overenthusiastic backstage correspondence at the Tony Awards, making me the first person to be made fun of for being too much of a theater nerd *at the Tony Awards.*[**]

[**] He profusely apologized so no need to give him more shit online for this.

couldn't even admit this cycle to myself—in the three-ish years that this plagued me, this was the only thing I ever wrote down about it in my diary:

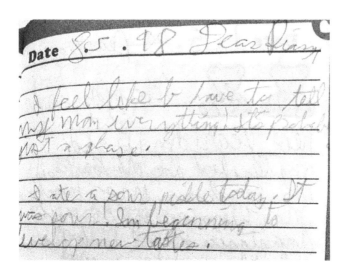

Date: *8-5-98*

Dear Diary, I feel like I have to tell my mom everything! *It's probably just a phase.*

(New paragraph to change the subject)

I ate a sour pickle today. It was sour! I'm beginning to develop new tastes.

If I couldn't even tell my own diary what was going on, I couldn't bring myself to tell this doctor. So when he asked me what was wrong, I said something to the effect of, "I just worry a lot." He asked me what I worry about. I sputtered and gave an answer that I'd seen normal kids give on TV shows: "School, homework, grades." He told me worrying was normal and that if I ever felt too overwhelmed with school pressure, I should just take some deep breaths. I said thank you and left his office. My parents asked how it went. I said I felt a lot better. It was a lie.

After refusing to tell the therapist my problems, I told myself that I'd stop confessing things to my parents. This made me fear any catalyst for a guilty thought so I tried to take preventive measures. I tried to avoid people touching me, because what if them touching me gave me a "funny feeling" down there and then I felt guilty about that?

Then came the day of the Fifth Grade Mother's Day Pageant. Mother's Day was that weekend, so the teacher decided to put on a show in the nearby park in which we would all perform poems and songs for our mothers. A few kids had been picked out to do some solo numbers; my crush Ethan (the class clown, more on him later) had written a very funny song called, "Mommy Mommy Mommy," which was mostly him strumming one chord on a guitar and just singing "Mommy Mommy Mommy" over and over again. It was of course, an unparalleled stroke of comedic brilliance.

I had written a song in the form of lyrics about how much I loved my mother to the tune of Pachelbel's Canon in D Major (the OTHER famous wedding song). I was watching a lot of the movie *Father of the Bride* around this time and it felt right.

It was lunchtime before we all had to walk over to the pageant, and it was just me, my teacher, and a girl named Molly in the classroom. I rummaged through my bag looking for a bobby pin. I said aloud, "What am I going to do with my hair?" But my teacher must have thought I'd said, "What am I going to wear?" because she said to me, "Oh, you're going to wear THAT?"

THAT was my usual outfit of sweatpants and a baggy shirt. I told her, um, yes, this is what I was wearing for the pageant. Was that a problem?

She suggested maybe I could have dressed in something nicer like how—she looked at Molly—how someone like Molly dressed. Molly was in a cute shirt and super-short white shorts. In a schoolmarm way I told the teacher that, no offense to Molly, I wouldn't wear shorts that short. Molly didn't know what to say and she left the room to avoid the situation entirely. My teacher said no, that's not what she meant, she didn't mean I LITERALLY had to dress like Molly, she just meant…oh, what did she mean? She searched for the correct words and then said:

"What I mean to say is…normal kids don't dress the way you do."

The room spun around me. I found some excuse to leave and headed straight for the bathroom. The door hadn't even closed before I started sobbing. And sobbing.

And sobbing.

My teacher had voiced everything I feared about myself. I wasn't normal. Something was deeply wrong with me. And an adult had said it, which made it true.

A few of my classmates walked in and asked me what was

wrong, and I told them what the teacher had said to me. In a moment of unity, one of the girls said to me, "Oh ignore her, she's a bitch." But that didn't help.

The moms were starting to arrive at the school for the pageant. Someone told my mother I was sobbing in the bathroom. She came in and I told her what happened.

I wasn't there when my mother ripped my teacher a new asshole, but I heard her shouting at her from inside the bathroom. Way to earn that pageant, Mom. Maybe some kids would have been embarrassed. But not me. I knew what this teacher did was wrong. I couldn't fight her myself, so I was happy to have an adult to take control.

My mom came back in the bathroom. I hugged her, thanked her, and told her I'd meet her with my class at the park. She asked me if I still wanted to do the pageant and I said yes, *the show must go on.*

Wiping my eyes, I rejoined my class while they gathered on the field. But my teacher told us all that she wanted to make a quick speech before we walked to the park. She then said, "You know, class, sometimes people say things that aren't nice. And instead of being upset, in those moments, you know what we need to do?"

I looked down. *Hi, ground. Please eat me. I'm ready.*

She continued. "We need to SHAKE IT OFF. That's right, we need to shake it off! Can everyone shake with me?"

And then, as if it were some sort of experimental theater exercise, everyone around me started to comically shake.

I will never forget the sound of them shaking. Like it was a joke. Like I was a joke.

I don't think any of the kids connected the weird shaking exercise to what had just happened between me and the teacher. But for many years after that, whenever I felt abnormal, I could almost hear the sound of my classmates shaking next to me.

The guilty thoughts finally started petering out in early seventh grade. By that point, I had started to confess a *lot* less when I realized intuitively that the confessions seemed to make the obsessions worse. (Which, incidentally, is exactly how OCD works.) Having run out of new guilty thoughts, obsessions veered into classic OCD territory. Not because I particularly feared germs or illness, but because my mind needed something new to obsess on. I washed my hands a lot and tried not to touch the area around the sink without a paper towel, you know, typical OCD fare. But honestly, my heart wasn't in it.

After the worst part of my OCD went away in eighth grade (why? I have no fucking idea),* my parents and I never discussed what happened. We all preferred to focus instead on the things that made me happy. And that, of course, was the arts. From middle school to college I learned that, as long as I was acting or singing or writing, I had to be present in the

---

* If you're a child psychologist and have any insights into my childhood OCD, tweet at me with the hashtag #diagnosechildrachel. No need to make it a dm. The more opinions, the better. You can reach me at the handle @tedcruz.

moment. I didn't have the mental space to be anxious. As long as I kept my mind engaged, everything would be okay. Whatever those thoughts were, they were gone and never to return again in any other form.

If this sentence seems ominous, that's because it is!

PART 3:
NORMAL PEOPLE HAVE HEALTHY RELATIONSHIPS

THE FUTURE MRS. NAZI

From the moment Mrs. Allen sat Ethan next to me so that I'd be a "good influence," I loved him and he hated me.

Ethan was the class clown of second grade. His parents were divorced so he always seemed like a messed-up "bad boy" to me, but until we shared a desk, I had no idea how laugh-out-loud funny he really was. In a project we had to do on the earth's biomes, he and I were assigned to do the "grasslands." As we were working on our presentation, he came up with the chant: "G-g-g-grasslands / We'll kick your asslands." It was scandalous, it was lewd, it was amazing. Remember the first time you saw *Borat* and you were like, "Well, my view of comedy is forever changed"? This was my that.

Shortly after our biomes project, I realized that I was desperately in love with him. I made no effort to hide my obsession. I went from being a studious goody two-shoes to a fidgety giggle monster. The chemicals of infatuation had taken

63

hold of my eight-year-old body and I was ready to throw away everything I'd worked for to be closer to him.

On his end, I'm pretty sure he saw me as a weirdo who laughed at his jokes and occasionally let him peer at my spelling test answers.

(Also, I should note that when I was eight, he was nine, which means he had all the power in the situation.)

I thought of him that whole summer, and when we came back for third grade, I ditched my own friends to be around him every snack and lunchtime. Realizing that he and his group of guy friends would never accept me as is, I made it my mission to fit in with them and become a "tomboy." Ethan and his friends were into basketball, so I got into basketball. (Well, the movie *Space Jam*, but that's basically the same thing.) Ethan and his friends liked the band 311, so I got into the band 311. (I mean, at least I said I liked 311 while secretly listening to the Spice Girls.) One day, Ethan and his friends stated that they would officially inaugurate me as a "tomboy." All I had to do was lick a rock. I did it. My social status with the group mildly improved.

Everything changed that Christmas when Ethan invited me to be his plus-one at a holiday party thrown by his after-school resource class. He told me that his mother made him invite me, but that didn't stop me from seeing it as our first date. When we were caught sharing a bag of candy, word traveled fast that we were "together," and I did nothing to quash the rumor. Surprisingly, this was a social disaster for a nine-year-old boy (who, to remind you, was technically older than I was so he had all the power in the situation).

After this fiasco, Ethan didn't want me hanging around him and his friends anymore. To get me to go away, he started making fun of me.

It began with light insults about me being a nerd and a dramatic dork (real original), but then he ramped it up in fourth grade. By that time, my obsessive thoughts had started, and I was starting to get teased for being weird. School was not a happy place, which meant I craved the high of being around Ethan even more. Of course, any association with me would bring Ethan even lower socially than he already was.

And that's when he resorted to getting straight up anti-Semitic.

When I say "anti-Semitic," I don't think Ethan really had anything against Jews. He knew and liked other members of my tribe—Manhattan Beach was pretty gentile, but it wasn't like one of those Jesus-ey Southern towns where people think Jews have horns or shit like that. So Ethan didn't have a reason to hate Jews, he just wanted to say anything to get me to go the fuck away. His innocent, childlike version of anti-Semitism meant that he'd say vaguely hateful things to me, like, "Look Rachel, there's Hitler over there!" and "Let's have a jump-the-Jew party!" Which really makes no sense, but, again, he was older than I was so he had all the power in the situation. One time, when I protested, he got really dark and said, "Don't be so sensitive, it's not my fault that if you lived in the forties you'd be in a gas chamber." (Ooooh, someone's been reading *The Berenstain Bears* and *Mein Kampf*!)

These remarks really tested my love for Ethan. I grew up in the type of Jewish household in which I didn't know a word of Hebrew, but I knew EVERY celebrity that had ever said anything anti-Semitic. Our Shabbat prayer was basically, "Baruch Atah Adonoi, Jesse Jackson, Vanessa Redgrave, Marlon Brando said 'kike' once." Torn between my love of Ethan and loyalty to my people, I reluctantly told my mother what Ethan said to me. Infuriated, she called his mother, who let out a resigned and unsurprised sigh.

Not even that stopped him from insulting me, so, while remaining deeply in love with Ethan, I told a teacher about him bullying me. This got Ethan in repeated detentions. Still wanting to be around him, though, I would full-on VISIT HIM IN DETENTION. I'd try to get him to apologize to me while saying things to him like, "You know, the Jews have contributed a lot of things to society." I'd say that getting him in detention and then visiting him in detention was fucked up, but, again, power, situation, he had.

All in all, my crush on Ethan lasted four years. It petered out in middle school when he and I didn't have any classes together. Absence can make the heart grow fonder, but, when you're twelve, it can also make the heart go, "Oh right, how's *that* guy doing?"

Thankfully, this fucked-up obsession with Ethan in no way set an unhealthy pattern for me in future relationships and hahahaahahahaha I can't even finish that sentence

INFATUATED LIKE A PRINCESS

Wrapped in infatuation
Whenever I see him
I dramatically swoop my arm with its elegant long sleeve
And royally swoon on a bed tapestried with velvet
As my crimson skirts collapse in a lake of self-pity
My corset wraps my ribs tight, bosom pulled
ravishingly up
Rose-red lips pucker in distress
As I think of my infatuation
I look a helpless beauty strewn across the bed
Furrowing my brow, fingering the heavy jewels around
my neck
While the picture of him glitters in my mind
—Myself, Age Fourteen

THE LAMEST MISTRESS: A FAIRY TALE

Once upon a time in a far-off kingdom, there lived a little princess. Her parents were destined to have just the one child because her father got a vasectomy shortly after she was born. As a result, she was adored, pampered, and protected behind the high walls of a gated community, which didn't make a lot of sense considering their town was already pretty safe, but whatever.

One day, the princess and her parents were dining at the food court of the local mall. It was a crowded day and, arms laden with Sbarro, they were lucky to find an empty table. Little did they know, the table had already been claimed by an old witch.

As they dug into their overcooked ziti, the witch approached. "Hey, that's my table! I claimed it!"

The parents of the princess replied, "Oh, sorry, we thought that was just some trash on it and we threw it awxay."

69

The witch screamed, "That was my ORANGE JULIUS!"

"The cup was basically empty."

"I was going to get a refill when I got back!"

Before the princess's parents could apologize, the old witch shook a gnarled finger, pointed it at the young princess, and laid a curse upon her. "From this day forward," she said, "your daughter will have a series of unhealthy relationships. Each relationship will be forbidden in its own way, but the reasons behind the relationship being forbidden won't be cool enough for her to make them sound like actual forbidden relationships when she relays the story to other people. The situations will be generally muddled and stupid. Thus, I curse your daughter to become . . . the world's lamest mistress."

The princess's parents were distraught. "Why, oh why would you do this, you evil witch?!"

The witch replied, "Well, to be fair, it'll be a mix of this curse and all of the natural causes of romantic obsession. See, romantic obsession, also known as 'limerence' as coined by the psychologist Dorothy Tennov, naturally feeds off the thrill of the chase, so anything with a 'forbidden' element is especially appealing. Limerence also makes your serotonin plummet and your daughter already has low serotonin due to mild depression inherited from both sides of the family so she'll be even more reliant on the dopamine surges caused by romantic love. BUT THE CURSE STILL PLAYS A BIG PART IN THIS HAHAHAHAHA!"

The princess ignored this whole exchange because she was

sack deep in a *Highlights* magazine word search and couldn't be bothered. Her desperate parents, though, asked the witch if there was any cure. The witch answered sagely, "Your daughter will have three great loves. When the fourth love comes along on her twenty-first birthday, she will have the chance to redeem herself. But if she fails, she is destined to remain alone forever."

And with that, the witch disappeared.

And then she reappeared in front of the Orange Julius stall. "One LARGE, please," she said very loudly in the direction of the princess's family.

The princess's parents mourned all day. But then Mark Harmon was Johnny Carson's guest that night on *The Tonight Show* and the princess's mother was a huge fan. The princess's parents fell asleep in front of the TV, and when they woke up the next morning, they forgot all about the incident with the witch.

So the princess grew up unaware of the curse placed over her head. And at the perfect fairy-tale-ey age of sixteen, it took hold.

For the princess had fallen in love with a duke she met during a summer teen production of the Gershwin tap musical *Crazy for You*. The duke's name was Brendan and, though he hadn't quite articulated it to himself yet, he was gay. However, this was not the reason their love was forbidden; this fact is just to show you that this first tale of forbidden love is already kind of half-assed at the outset.

One day, Brendan the duke wanted to ask the princess to go to a movie, but he couldn't reach her cell, so he called her house. He had spotty cell service, which resulted in him repeatedly calling her house, her mother picking up, Brendan cursing at the service being spotty and then hanging up. After this happened five times, the princess's mother thought Brendan was prank-calling the house. Denouncing him as a hoodlum, she forbade the princess to hang out with him.

I would say this is when the princess and the duke's secret love affair began, but, in actuality, they were still just friends at this point. So their forbidden "romance" was just two platonic friends sneaking around to listen to obscure show tunes and see musicals done by local private performing arts high schools, after which they'd lament the fact that their respective public high school theater programs really needed to step it up.

It wasn't until they did another show together that they actually started dating, which made the whole "sneaking around thing" a lot more exciting, even though the only thing they'd do in these secret trysts was basically what they did before, except now there was tongue. One time, they did go a little further in a movie theater on Christmas while watching the Paul Giamatti hit *Sideways*, but the duke wanted to stop a few minutes in because "this movie is really interesting." There were many other signs that the duke might not have been into women—his believable turn as the Emcee in *Cabaret*, his "notes" on her kissing technique, and the fact that everyone said, "Hey, you know your boyfriend's gay, right?"

And then the princess's parents discovered her with the duke and locked her high in a tower guarded by a fierce dragon.

Nah, just kidding. The relationship ended naturally when the duke went to a summer musical theater program at Carnegie Mellon and broke up with the princess to "keep his options open."

And somewhere far away, the witch let out a cackle. The first lame forbidden relationship had ended.[*]

𝕿he story of the second great love:

The princess was in another teen musical production. This time, it was a show called *Into the Woods*, and she was, ironically, playing "The Witch." Not "The Witch" that cursed her in this story but another witch in another story, which is the story *Into the Woods*. If you're confused, blame it on the witch. Not the musical witch, the witch witch.

Moving on, the princess was the lead in the musical and that's all you really need to know. Now, as with any Sondheim work, the music of *Into the Woods* is incredibly complicated and needed a proficient musical director to guide these young teens. And thus, Sir Patrick entered the princess's life.

Sir Patrick was a Young Knight from the far-off kingdom of the San Gabriel Valley. He was only a year older than the princess, but, as established in a previous story, that

---

[*] For the record, Brendan and I are best friends and, for that reason, he is the only love interest besides my husband who doesn't have an alias in this book. My husband actually did request the alias of "Colonel Pennyfeather." His request was not honored.

technically meant he had all the power in the situation. More important, he had been renowned in the Southern California regional theater circle as a "musical prodigy" so he was brought on to be the music director of this production. Sir Patrick was obsessed with the work of Stephen Sondheim and also, shockingly, tits?

With the princess playing the most complex role in the show, she and Sir Patrick started to spend a lot of time together. Despite the fact that the princess had a boyfriend at the time (no, not Brendan the Duke, a different guy, it's a whole thing), the princess soon fell madly in love with the dashing musical director Knight. The two of them would talk on the phone until 2:00 a.m. about art and music and Sondheim's recurring motif of "the Bean Theme," after which the princess would masturbate and then fall asleep so quickly that she'd wake up the next morning with her hand still in her underwear. Then, the night of the cast party, she and Sir Patrick kissed.

And thus, the second forbidden romance began.

The next two months were a whirlwind. The princess didn't want her friends or parents to know that she and Sir Patrick had fallen in love due to the fact he was kind of an authority figure even though the show was over. And did I mention he was a YEAR older?

Thus the princess and Sir Patrick made out in his big white van all over town. Why a white van? It was good for holding instruments but is also a fun detail for this story because it's creepy. Anyway, for three solid months, the princess and Sir

Patrick got to first base + nipples (also known as "second base") every chance they could get.

Everything was bliss until, one day, they were discovered. Sir Patrick was thrown into a dungeon and the princess was so distraught that she jumped into the ocean and turned into sea foam.

Okay not really, but wouldn't that be cool?

What really happened was that Sir Patrick was a drummer and he went on tour with a band. The princess didn't hear from him all summer and when he got back he told her he'd "changed a lot" on tour and wasn't interested in a relationship anymore but was still really attracted to the princess and was wondering if they could continue to "hook up" with "no strings." The princess said she was "totally chill with that" and they made out on and off for the next two months until Sir Patrick stopped texting her altogether because he most likely found a girl who would blow him.

And thus, the second forbidden romance reached its conclusion.

Boy, what a lame fairy tale, right? Want me to make things lamer? The relationship with Sir Patrick never really ended. For the next two years, Sir Patrick would make out with the princess then say it shouldn't happen anymore then text her to hook up whenever he was high. This relationship even extended into the princess's freshman year of college. Sir Patrick was going to be in New York with his band and, knowing that the princess was a virgin, went on an active sexting campaign to convince her to fuck him while he was visiting. Since talking dirty to a virgin is as hot as it sounds ("What do you want me to do to you?" "I want you to…look at…my vagina and…describe it"), the princess agreed to lose her virginity to Sir Patrick. She bought condoms, lube, and a pretty new green dress to get fucked in. However, when Sir Patrick actually came to New York he claimed to be so sick that he was "coughing up blood" so they shouldn't kiss. When he roughly fingered her too hard and she said "Ow," he had a sudden crisis of conscience and announced he "couldn't do this" because she was a "good kid."

Then the princess went to see his band play that night anyway, after which she smoked her first cigarette to make her lungs hurt as much as her heart.

Let's move on to the third love.

Ugh. This part is even more complicated.

Once upon a time, again, in a far-off kingdom, again, the princess joined a sketch comedy group at New York University. Being a naive little princess who thought herself to be an unlovable dork (see: the previous two stories), she was unaware of the universal truth that if you're vaguely funny, vaguely attractive, and vaguely have a vagina, men in comedy will find you very appealing. This often leads to numerous men being into the same girl but being too awkward to handle it maturely. Ask any young comedy princess and, chances are, she will have stories of multiple suitors, duels fought in her name, and glorious balls (both the dance kind and the testicle kind, but either way, both smell of PBR and mildew).

So the princess joined the sketch group and immediately caught the eye of, not one, but two...earls. These earls were older guys in the college sketch comedy group and we'll call them, respectively, the Earl of Chuckleshire and the Earl of Laffland. These two earls were not only best friends but also comedy writing partners. This is going to end well.

Our princess was pursued by the Earl of Laffland her freshman year and they dated for a bit, but then he turned distant and they broke up. A few months later, the Earl of Chuckleshire moved on in, which made the Earl of Laffland (again, his best friend and comedy writing partner) very jealous. Whether this jealousy came from him still caring for the princess or if it came from jealousy over the Earl of Chuckleshire having more "industry heat" due to his spec script of *Futurama* landing him some general meetings, who's to say. Whatever the cause, the Earl of Laffland went on an active campaign to steal back the princess.

The princess was very confused because, at nineteen years old, she was being pursued by two of her comedy mentors. She had feelings for both of them, but it was unclear if these feelings were genuine or if they came from the fact the men were older and funnier and kind of authority figures and also one of them owned something called a wine rack?!

Meanwhile, the princess was now a sophomore in college and both of the earls had since graduated from her sketch comedy group. Upon their graduation, they had named her the group's assistant director to eventually ascend to the role of director. The princess started to feel like this whole earl drama was getting in the way of her leadership duties, so she did the mature thing and called off everything with both earls.

Aaaand that lasted for about a week because she went to the Earl of Chuckleshire's apartment to pick up a belt she'd left there and then they fucked. And then after that she continued to get texts from the Earl of Laffland so they kept hanging out, which led to secret kissy kissy time.

Inevitably, the Earl of Chuckleshire found out about this secret kissy kissy time. And for the first instance in this story that actually feels like a fairy tale, his heart shattered in a million pieces. The girl he still cared for was hooking up with his best friend and comedy partner. Ignoring the fact the Earl of Laffland was complicit in this, the princess blamed herself and felt terrible about how she had treated the Earl of Chuckleshire.

Until, that is, the Earl of Chuckleshire reached out to the current director of the sketch group and asked him to strip the princess of her "assistant director" title as punishment. To be clear: The princess was no longer assistant director of her sketch comedy group because she was in a love triangle with two people who'd already graduated. And then she was instructed by the current director to tell everyone else on the group that she quit being assistant director because she "couldn't handle the workload."

In later life, the princess would realize this was kiiiiiiinda "sexual harassment." But at the time, she just thought she deserved exactly what she got. She was in the midst of the deepest depression of her life when the Earl of Laffland reached out to her to keep seeing each other in secret. He said he couldn't live without her. And the princess believed him because, at that point, she felt as if his love was all she had left.

So now the princess was in a secret relationship with the Earl of Laffland because she didn't want to cause any more drama between her boyfriend and his writing partner...or something like that? The reasoning is foggy but listen, you don't earn the title of being "the lamest mistress" without being a mistress for a lame reason.

The Earl of Laffland and the princess swore their love to each other. And that's not exaggerating for a fairy-tale-ey effect; they really were head over heels. The princess spent her days in a depressed agony, living only for the nights in which she could get on the A train express to the last stop in Washington Heights and be at the apartment of her true love. And every night, the earl told her their love wouldn't have to be a secret for much longer. Soon he'd tell his friend, and then they could tell the whole world.

But then one day the condom broke. And as they stood in line at the local drugstore to get the morning-after pill, the princess felt the earl's gaze grow cold. She knew in her heart that the whole thing had just gotten too real for him. And over the next few months, just like Sir Patrick, the earl began to...just...fade away. His texts and calls slowed down to a trickle then stopped altogether. He avoided her gaze whenever they were in the same room. A few months later, the princess called the earl to ask what the deal was. The earl told her that he and Chuckleshire had some interest in a script they'd written together so he and the princess probably could never happen. She also found out he had started dating someone else.

At this point, the princess had lost not only her literal love, but her love of comedy. She remained on the sketch group for some reason, but every rehearsal or show reminded her of her shortcomings as a person.

And thousands of miles away, the witch was ecstatic. The princess lost her third love and the curse had fully come to pass.

But then the witch remembered the loophole she built into the curse. Oh right, she remembered, something about a fourth love redeeming it all? "Fuck, why did I do that?" the witch said to herself. "Oh well, she's bound to screw it up." Honestly, the witch's spite after all these years toward the princess was baffling considering it was, at the end of the day, all just over a food court table and some Orange Julius. But, witches gonna witch.

And then, just as the princess was at her most despondent... she met a handsome prince!

(Well, not met. She'd known the prince for a long time. But sure, for the purpose of this story, this is when they "met."*)

---

* In general, the princess recommends that this is the best way to meet someone. Wait, it's clear in this story that I'm the princess, right?

This handsome prince was unlike any of the loves that had come beforehand. First, he was definitely attracted to women. That was a plus. Second, he wasn't in a position of authority over her, another plus. And third, when the princess was around him, she was the best and most authentic version of herself.

Yet the princess was scared to take things further with the prince. Her love life had been so weird and terrible up until this point. What if she ruined it like she inevitably ruined everything? While visiting home one day, she mentioned to her parents that, when it came to love, it felt as if she was...cursed.

"Oh, right!" her parents said. "We TOTALLY forgot to tell you about this witch in a mall..." and they relayed the whole story about the curse. Afterward, the princess stared at them in shocked silence. Her parents filled the silence with, "So yeah, now you know!"

The princess was furious. "HOW did you not tell me this?"

"Eh, I think Mark Harmon was on Carson that night?" her parents replied.

The princess went to her room, turned on the calming sounds of the Broadway soundtrack to *The Full Monty*, and thought about everything. She thought about her feelings for the prince and the other men she'd loved. So she was right. She HAD been cursed. It HADN'T been her fault. And now all she had to do was fall in love with the handsome prince and it would be fine! The curse would be broken!

But no, that wasn't right. As the princess thought about

every lame and weird romantic situation over the course of her short life, she realized that there was always a cure for the curse right in front of her the whole time: opting out. At any point, the princess could have left each of these relationships, but she didn't. The problem wasn't who she fell in love with, the problem was how she stayed in unhappy situations long after the writing was on the wall. She had let herself be controlled by a combination of romantic obsession and her own lack of self-esteem. The princess looked in the mirror and said, "I am worth more than this curse says I am."

And with that, the curse was broken. And she let out a huge fart.

She knew that she still had to work on the relationship with the prince and that her problems were far from over. But from that point forward, she vowed to put her own happiness before pleasing someone else. And even when she married the prince, she still saw it as just a step in her own happiness, not a

Happily Ever After.

PART 4:

NORMAL PEOPLE DON'T DO THEATER

HOW CAN I EXPLAIN?

Ever since the brave Thespis stepped out of the chorus to become the world's first actor, people have been shouting back, "Yo, Thespis, why don't you play sports instead, you fucking dork?!" before throwing rotten spanakopita at him.

In case it's not already apparent: I am a theater kid. For most of my life, I loved everything about the theater (spelled "theatre" if you're *that guy*). I loved that moment right before the house lights went down and the overture started, the ecstatic rush of watching a good tap number set on a boat, the moment Mimi almost dies in Roger's arms but then she comes back to life and they sing a reprise of "There's Only Us" and you're like OMG yes I knew she couldn't die I knew it. And of course, I loved the attention. Oh boy, did I *really* love the attention.

But the thing I loved most about theater(re) was that being a theater kid was an easy explanation for the reason I didn't fit in. It meant that I was a cultured and misunderstood eccentric whose interests made me wise beyond my years. I never had to actually question my actions, my choices, or the deeper reasons for my unhappiness—being a theater kid simply meant my problems were all caused by it being me vs. everyone else. Even when I did plays (in the form of rinky-dink children's community theater productions), I was with other kids who *did* theater but weren't *theater kids*, you know? They didn't live and breathe theater like me. I remember one pretty girl in one of those plays talking backstage about the highlights she just got in her hair at a local salon and I thought, What a phony popular bitch. Get out of here. You don't need the theater and it doesn't need you.

This narrative had to shift when I *did* befriend other actual "theater kids." Finding my fellow die hards through my high school theater department and summer teen theater productions was great but it meant I had to rejigger the way I blamed theater for all my problems. Now I told myself that theater was my LIFE and everything else had to be secondary to it. My studies hadn't slipped because I had some fundamental problems staying focused in school—I'd just rather be rehearsing! (I even had a shirt that said, I'D RATHER BE REHEARSING. And the necklace. And the jacket. And the bag. And the socks. And a backup shirt.) I was constantly tired not because I had trouble regulating my sleep and setting boundaries for myself—I was just a night owl meant to be sipping martinis at Sardi's while everyone else was snoozin'!

The best thing about blaming every problem on theater was

that there was always hope of the "someday." I told myself that as soon as I could pursue theater full-time in that distant "someday," all of my problems would disappear.

And then I actually started pursuing theater full-time and I realized that was bullshit.

Theater didn't solve any of my problems. In fact, it made some of my problems worse.

Hmm, how can I explain...Oh, I know!

Rachel Bloom

HOW CAN I EXPLAIN?

A Very Rushed and Truncated Musical About My Relationship with Musicals (That Glosses Over Some Things but Gives You a General Idea of My Trajectory)

Note: To listen along to the musical as you read it, you can visit racheldoesstuff.com.

EXT. AN ADULT COMMUNITY THEATER PRODUCTION OF *GUYS AND DOLLS*—TORRANCE, CALIFORNIA—1992— EVENING

A happy audience of mostly senior citizens streams out of a community center. An upbeat tune begins. They sing:

        OLD-ASS AUDIENCE MEMBERS
WASN'T THAT SWEET?
THAT WAS NICE.
LIVE THEATER AT A REASONABLE PRICE.
CATCHY TUNES
I COULD HUM EVERY NOTE!
NOW LET'S GO HOME AND WATCH *MURDER, SHE WROTE*!

I WANT TO BE WHERE THE NORMAL PEOPLE ARE

Among the senior citizens exiting the theater, a little girl walks with her GRANDPARENTS. This little girl is me, RACHEL BLOOM. She wears polka-dot shorts and sparkly red shoes like Dorothy from *The Wizard of Oz* because, of course she does. Rachel clutches her *Guys and Dolls* program and sings:

> YOUNG RACHEL BLOOM
> THAT'S WHAT I WANT TO DO!
> THAT'S ALL I WANT TO DO AND WHO I WANT TO BE!
> THAT'S WHAT I WANT TO DO!
> BROADWAY IS THE PLACE FOR ME!

> YOUNG RACHEL BLOOM
> Grandma and Grandpa, I wanna start doing community theater!

> GRANDPARENTS
> Sure!

ADOLESCENT RACHEL BLOOM enters. She wears her entire I'D RATHER BE REHEARSING ensemble.

> ADOLESCENT RACHEL BLOOM
> Hi! I'm older now!

THAT'S *STILL* WHAT I WANT TO DO!
I DON'T CARE IF IT MAKES ME STRANGE.

BOTH RACHEL BLOOMS
THAT'S WHAT WE WANT TO DO!
AND SHOOT US IN THE HEAD
IF OUR AMBITIONS SHOULD EVER CHANGE!

THE DUMBFUCK BULLY CHORUS (AKA THE GASKINS) enter. They mock both Rachels.

THE GASKINS
FUCK YOU, YOU STUPID FREAKS
WE'RE BACK FROM PART 1.
FUCK YOU, YOU FREAKY BROADWAY FREAKS
ON THE COUNT OF THREE YOU'LL BE SHUNNED.
THREE!

As the Gaskins repeat this chorus, the Rachels sing in counterpoint:

BOTH RACHEL BLOOMS
THAT'S WHAT WE WANT TO DO.
NO ONE GETS WHY IT MAKES US WHOLE.
THAT'S WHAT WE WANT TO DO.

I WANT TO BE WHERE THE NORMAL PEOPLE ARE

THE TAUNTING ONLY PUSHES US FURTHER
TOWARD OUR GOAL!

Song ends. The Gaskins and Young Rachel leave the stage. Young Rachel shuffles off to Buffalo as she exits. The Gaskins try to trip her.

                    ADOLESCENT RACHEL BLOOM
No one will ever understand me and that's the way it has to be. I am an underdog whose sheer talent will someday prove everyone wrong. And then they'll all be sorry. *(pause, then)* Just to be clear, I mean that they'll be sorry in an "I'm gonna be successful" way, not in a Columbine way.

A BUNCH OF FLYERS come down from the ceiling.

                    ADOLESCENT RACHEL BLOOM
What's this? Our school's beloved drama and English teacher is starting a YEAR-ROUND MUSICAL THEATER CLASS? Wow, I'll finally get to spend all of my time doing theater instead of just little community productions

91

in the summer? This class sounds amazing!

A happy waltz begins and the Gaskins reenter.

                    THE GASKINS
BECAUSE   THAT   TEACHER   SAID   THEATER   IS
COOOOOOOL
ITS EXISTENCE WILL NOW BE TOLERATED IN THIS
SCHOOOOOOOOL.

MORE STUDENTS enter.

                    ALL STUDENTS
THIS CLASS IS NOW THE HIPPEST PLACE TO
BEEEEEEE
SO WE WILL ALL RESPECT THE PEOPLE WHO GET
THE LEEEEEEEADS!
ACTING, SINGING, DANCING, WHAT A THRIIII-
IILL!
BUT WHAT LOSER WOULD HAVE HAD THE TIME TO
HONE THOSE SKIIIIIILLS?!

Rachel raises her hand enthusiastically!

I WANT TO BE WHERE THE NORMAL PEOPLE ARE

                    ADOLESCENT RACHEL BLOOM
Um, THIS BITCH!

Song ends. THE TEACHER enters.

                         THE TEACHER
That's right, that bitch! While the rest of
you were going to parties and tonguing each
other's mouth holes, little lonely Rachel
here was honing her craft! And now, I dub
her . . . the lead in everything!

Everyone looks at Rachel admiringly. A "The
Wizard and I"-sounding song begins.

                    ADOLESCENT RACHEL BLOOM
THEY LIKE ME NOW
NOT IN SPITE OF WHO I AM
BUT BECAUSE OF IT.
THEY LIKE ME NOW
I WAS RIGHT ALL ALONG
AND THEY WERE FULL OF SHIT.

Rachel stuffs her bra.

                ADOLESCENT RACHEL BLOOM
Time has passed! I'm in high school now and
a B cup!
NOW I FEEL A CHANGE HAPPENING TO ME.
I'M NO LONGER HATED.
SURE, I'M STILL NOT POPULAR
BUT AT LEAST I'M TOLERATED!
(key change)
TOLERATED!

The Bullies circle Rachel with giant feathers.

                ADOLESCENT RACHEL BLOOM
THEY LIKE ME NOW
AND WITH THIS
I FEEL A REBIRTH.
THEY LIKE ME NOW
WHICH GOES TO SHOW
MY TALENT IS SYNONYMOUS WITH MY SELF-WORTH!

She gets an acceptance letter.

                ADOLESCENT RACHEL BLOOM
Wow, I got into NYU, Tisch School of the
Arts! This confirms my trajectory!

I WANT TO BE WHERE THE NORMAL PEOPLE ARE

COLLEGE RACHEL BLOOM walks in. Her boobs are even bigger.

> COLLEGE RACHEL BLOOM
> Tagging you out, adolescent me! We're in college now and the freshman fifteen has made us a C cup!

Adolescent Rachel Bloom leaves; College Rachel picks up the song.

> COLLEGE RACHEL BLOOM
> YES MY TALENT IS SYNONYMOUS WITH MY SELF-WORTH!

A bunch of other COLLEGE-AGED KIDS walk in and join Rachel for the big finish.

> RACHEL AND COLLEGE KIDS
> MY TALENT IS SYNONYMOUS WITH MY SELF-WOOOOOOORTH!

Song ends.

95

COLLEGE RACHEL BLOOM
Sorry, who are all of you?

CLASSMATE #1
Oh, we're your new classmates in the musical theater program at Tisch!

CLASSMATE #2
Like you, we were ALSO outcasts and ALSO the leads of all the musicals!

COLLEGE RACHEL BLOOM
Oh cool! It's my tribe! Let's all be friends!

CLASSMATE #3
Hmm, that's gonna be tough since a lot of us already know each other from elite arts summer camps on the East Coast!

CLASSMATE #4
We should also add that a lot of us are straight-up more talented than you are.

CLASSMATE #5
Get ready to feel threatened!

I WANT TO BE WHERE THE NORMAL PEOPLE ARE

CLASSMATE #6

And did we mention that our personalities
are insufferable?

CLASSMATE #7

Oh hey, guys! I found a piano! Let's all
sing and compare voices!

ALL CLASSMATES

Yay! / That's my favorite thing to do!
/ People tell me I sound like Kristin
Chenoweth! / People tell me that, too! /
Kristin Chenoweth is my aunt! / et cetera.

As the classmates compare voices, a SONG BEGINS.
Vibe of this song: fifteen feral cats being
bludgeoned to death with a Tony Award.

ALL CLASSMATES

HOW HIGH CAN YOU BELT?
HOW HIGH CAN YOU BELT?
YOU CAN WEAR YOUR TALENT LIKE A PELT
WHEN WE JUDGE HOW HIGH YOU CAN BELT!

With each new line, the key changes.

                    CLASSMATE #1
        I CAN BELT THIIIIS!

                    CLASSMATE #2
        I CAN BELT THIIIIIS!

                    CLASSMATE #3
        WELL I CAN BELT THIIIIIS!

                    CLASSMATE #4
        I CAN BELT THIIIIS!

                    CLASSMATE #5
        WELL I CAN BELT THIIIIS!

                COLLEGE RACHEL BLOOM
        AND I CAN BELT THI—

It's too high for her. She dissolves into a
coughing fit. Her classmates awkwardly leave
the stage.

                COLLEGE RACHEL BLOOM
        Okay, so maybe these aren't my people,

I WANT TO BE WHERE THE NORMAL PEOPLE ARE

per se. But they won't distract me from
the reason I was here in the first place:
to celebrate the glory of musical theater!

College Rachel puts on a headset and sits in
front of a light board.

COLLEGE RACHEL BLOOM
And I'm in luck because, as a freshman, I
get to run lights for a new musical being
done by the older kids! It's based on the
Greek play *Lysistrata*! And it's a . . .

CHORUS sings from offstage to the tune of the
Jaws theme.

CHORUS
NEW WORK.

COLLEGE RACHEL BLOOM
That's right! When you go to school in NYC,
you get to be on the forefront of musical
theater and watch—

                    CHORUS
NEW WORK.

              COLLEGE RACHEL BLOOM
Why are you singing it ominously like that?

                    CHORUS
NEW WORK NEW WORK NEW WORK NEW WORK . . .

The Chorus walk in all dressed in togas and
act out this musical based on *Lysistrata*. It's
basically a bunch of gratuitously sexual jazz
choreography. Adolescent Rachel, Young Rachel,
and the Bullies enter like a Greek chorus and
solemnly chant in unison:

              RACHEL GREEK CHORUS
  And it was then that Rachel realized
  Upon seeing this dogshit musical
  That "new work" is always a crapshoot.
  And unlike other dogshit musicals from her
  past
  She couldn't walk out at intermission
  Or throw away the cast album
  And never think of it again.
  She just had to sit there

I WANT TO BE WHERE THE NORMAL PEOPLE ARE

Night after night
Watching it
And Watching It
And Watching It
Hitting the lights at the end of each song
To match a comedic "bump" in the music
That told the audience that what they just
watched was supposed to be "funny."

Rachel throws down her headset.

                COLLEGE RACHEL BLOOM
Okay, so I feel disenchanted with musical
theater as a whole plus the talents of my
classmates threaten me on a daily basis. This
BFA thing wasn't what I thought it was gonna
be. I need to do some serious soul searching.

Music note: Ding! College Rachel gets an idea.

                COLLEGE RACHEL BLOOM
OR, I could just . . .

Upbeat music kicks in!

                    COLLEGE RACHEL BLOOM
    NOT TRY!
    NOT TRY AT ALL!

We montage her through each class. She half-
asses everything.

                    COLLEGE RACHEL BLOOM
    SHOWING UP LATE
    MAKES ME FEEL GREAT.
    NOT LEARNING MY LINES
    OOH, IT FEELS SO FINE
    WHEN YOU DO NOT TRY!
    NOT TRY AT ALL!
    BECAUSE GOD FORBID I WORKED MY HARDEST
    AND DOUBLED DOWN ON BEING AN ARTIST
    AND I STILL WASN'T THE BEST.
    THE THOUGHT GIVES ME A PAIN IN MY CHEST.
    SO IT'S BETTER TO
    NOT TRY
    NOT TRY AT ALL
    THAN HAVE TO FACE SOME
    COLD
    HARD
    TRUUUUUUTHS!

Song ends. A BUNCH OF FLYERS once again come
down from the ceiling.

> COLLEGE RACHEL BLOOM
> Ceiling flyers again? That's a convenient
> plot device.

> AUTHOR RACHEL BLOOM (V.O.)
> Shut up and read it.

College Rachel reads a flyer.

> COLLEGE RACHEL BLOOM
> "Auditions for a sketch comedy group"? Hmm.
> That sounds interesting.

COMEDY GUY enters.

> COMEDY GUY
> Cool, you auditioned and got into the sketch
> comedy group!

> COLLEGE RACHEL BLOOM
> Wow, that fast?

COMEDY GUY

I mean, we could do a musical number that shows you auditioning for the sketch comedy group and then getting called back for the sketch comedy group but that seems really boring.

COLLEGE RACHEL BLOOM

Yeah, that would be like the baseball glove song in *Dear Evan Hansen*. Like, who cares?

COLLEGE GUY

Hey there, that musical won't come out for another thirteen years!

COLLEGE RACHEL BLOOM

Oopsies, you're right! Hey, I just realized— you're really funny!

COLLEGE GUY

And you can be, too!

COLLEGE RACHEL BLOOM

But how?

COLLEGE GUY launches into a ballad. His voice
is bad.

> COLLEGE GUY
ARE YOU TIRED OF YOUR LIFE BEING IN FLUX?
DOES IT MAKE YOU WANT TO NOT GIVE TWO FUCKS?

Rachel nods.

> COLLEGE GUY
TOO MUCH CHANGE, TOO MUCH TO QUESTION!
LET ME MAKE A WEE SUGGESTION:
'STEAD OF WORRYING 'BOUT YOUR PROBLEMS BIG
AND SMALL
TRY AN ART FORM IN WHICH PEOPLE DO NOT
CHANGE AT ALL.

> COLLEGE RACHEL BLOOM
And what art form is that?

> COLLEGE GUY
Sketch comedy, of course!

A romantic waltz begins.

Rachel Bloom

COLLEGE GUY

SKETCH IS THE ART OF THINGS STAYING THE SAME.
THAT SAMENESS GETS BIGGER AND THAT'S CALLED
"THE GAME."
THE GAME IS THE PATTERN OF WHAT'S FUNNY AND
GREAT.
FROM THIS COMEDY MATH YOU MUST NOT DEVIATE.

SAY YOU'RE WRITING A SKETCH CALLED "TIME
TRAVELING PENIS."
IT'D START IN A TIME MACHINE WITH A PHALLIC
MATH GENIUS.
THEN HE'D GO TO ANCIENT ROME TO JIZZ ALL
OVER CAESAR
THEN ON TO THE YEAR 4000 IN WHICH HE'D SAY
"GEE, SIR,
"WHERE ARE THE VAGINAS?" AND A ROBOT REPLIES
"GONE.
"WOMEN HAVE BEEN OUTLAWED AND NO ONE MAKES
SPAWN."
SO THE PENIS FUCKS THE ROBOT
ET CETERA, YOU GET IT.
IT'S A PENIS WHO TIME TRAVELS.
THAT'S THE GAME, DON'T FORGET IT.

SKETCH IS THE ART OF THINGS STAYING THE SAME.
IF YOU'RE STILL CONFUSED, LET ME EXPLAIN:

IF THE TIME TRAVELING PENIS DECIDES HE'S
UNHAPPY
AND ALL THE TIME TRAVELING MAKES HIM FEEL
CRAPPY
SO HE SETTLES DOWN, FINDS A WIFE, HAS TWO KIDS
THEN WE DON'T KNOW ANYMORE WHAT THE SKETCH IS.

COLLEGE RACHEL BLOOM
RIGHT, 'CAUSE ONCE THE SKETCH BECOMES PLOTTY,
THE FUNNY IS GONE.

BOTH
THERE'S NO REASON FOR THE SKETCH TO KEEP
GOING ON!

COLLEGE RACHEL BLOOM
Wow, I get it! Sketch is the art of explor-
ing the stasis of a situation. Besides this
being a calming metaphor for the stasis I
crave in my life right now, this structure
actually really gives me some organiza-
tional principles to creativity I've never
had before. Plus, the more I do comedy the
more I realize a lot of what I used to
find "funny" in musical theater is dated
and cheesy! So fuck musical theater, I'm in
love with sketch writing!

COLLEGE GUY

And fuck YOU, you fucked my friend!

COLLEGE RACHEL BLOOM

What?

COLLEGE GUY

See the previous chapters, I gotta run, you're dead to me and on your own now, byeeeeeeeeee!

He FLIES away.

COLLEGE RACHEL BLOOM

I don't know what to do. I thought musical theater was my everything but that wasn't right. Then I thought sketch comedy was my everything but now it makes me sad and also guys in comedy can be fucking assholes so maybe that wasn't right, either.

Young Rachel Bloom and Adolescent Rachel Bloom reenter.

I WANT TO BE WHERE THE NORMAL PEOPLE ARE

                    YOUNG RACHEL BLOOM
Don't forget what we always said about
Broadway!

Both Rachels sing a REPRISE of the first song.

                      BOTH RACHELS
THAT'S WHAT WE WANT TO DO.
WE DON'T CARE IF IT MAKES US STRANGE.

College Rachel joins in because it's a reprise
and she has to.

                      ALL RACHELS
THAT'S WHAT WE WANT TO DO!
AND SHOOT US IN THE HEAD
IF OUR AMBITIONS SHOULD EVER CHANGE!

                   COLLEGE RACHEL BLOOM
But wait. They HAVE changed. I'm in a state
of flux. But maybe that's good.

During the following inspirational monologue, Young Rachel and Adolescent Rachel sadly raise two guns and point them at each other's heads.

COLLEGE RACHEL BLOOM

I put a lot of pressure on musical theater to be my saving grace. And when that didn't work, I put the same amount of pressure on sketch comedy. I keep bouncing from extreme to extreme and, huh, that can't be good. You know what? I'm only twenty-one years old and I have time to try a bunch of different things. So maybe I'll keep doing comedy and theater and see how it goes and stop putting pressure on myself to decide what to do and who to be *right at this very moment*. Right, guys?

College Rachel turns around to see Young Rachel and Adolescent Rachel pointing guns at each other. No one knows what to do. College Rachel turns to the audience and gasps like Eliza at the end of *Hamilton* because that's as good a way to end a show as any.

END OF MUSICAL

THE BIG AUDITION!

Auditioning for college theater programs was one of the most stressful times in my life. With so much competition for so few programs, the question you must ask yourself is: How can I stand out from the pack? The answer is to find the right audition monologue. You need to find something that grabs them from moment one, something edgy, something brave, and something that shows off your complete range in a short amount of time. Sure, you could look through those monologue audition books, or you could just use the following:

The Greatest College Audition Monologue in the World

IT'S NOT MY FAULT, IMOGEN. It's not my fault that I am the BEST ACTRESS IN THE WORLD. It's not my FAULT that I can transition seamlessly from an *(do all of the following accents and dialects)* Irish dialect to British to Russian to Jamaican to Australian to Southern Belle. And it's not my FAULT that every college I auditioned for wanted me. *(Take a second to look at each audition proctor directly.)*

You know what? I don't have time for your bullshit today. I need to practice my *(choose one or pick your own special skill)* juggling / ribbon dancing / martial arts / banjo / acrobatics / Filipino stick dancing. *(Begin doing special skill and keep doing it throughout the rest of the monologue.)* Oh, what, Imogen, you're pissed that I'm practicing my *(insert special skill again)* while we're talking? It's called a SPECIAL SKILL and I need to hone it every day because I CARE about my CRAFT.

I know what this is really about. You're angry because I had that ABORTION. That's right. I said it. ABORTION. Yeah, I'm not afraid to say that and other edgy things out loud. ISRAEL. GENTRIFICATION. THE DEATH OF THE AMERICAN DREAM. INSTAGRAM ADDICTION. REPUBLICANS. BULIMIA. 4CHAN.

Remember how it was, Imogen? Remember when we loved each other? Remember when we had lesbian sex so passionately that we BLED? That's right, we BLED. I don't know the mechanics of what caused it, but we BLED. And my blood mixed with your blood and it formed a super blood that could take over the world and spread peace and love but also anger and justice. *(Stop doing special skill and start crying with real tears.)* But now it's over. You've ripped it to shreds. Are you happy, Imogen? ARE. YOU. HAPPY?! *(Dry tears with open palm of hand then launch into the final part.)* I'm gonna tell you the truth. And the truth is. YOU'RE NOT GOOD ENOUGH TO PLAY OPHELIA.

A BIT OF FANFICTION

Being a theater kid still colors the way I see the world. Every time I take in a piece of art about middle or high school, I wonder what the theater kids are up to in that world. And since I love the Harry Potter fanfiction community,[*] I present to you now:

---

[*] I wrote the bulk of this book from August 2019 to early March 2020. I have tried to leave what I wrote unaltered as a sort of time capsule of my life before March 2020 (see: afterword), but I would be remiss if I didn't acknowledge J. K. Rowling's disappointing comments about trans people that she tweeted a few months after. Since I still have such admiration for the HP fanfiction writing community and love for my fellow Potterheads, I decided to keep this story in. And also, I've wanted to write this story for like ten years and I'm really proud of it and she doesn't get a dime from a parody being published so that's good, but man, it's really complicated to be a Harry Potter fan right now because it's so inextricable from my generation's sense of identity yet the shit she's saying fucking sucks. Ugh.

HARRY POTTER AND THE HOGWARTS DRAMA CLUB

Note: The following story takes place during Book 6, Harry Potter and the Half-Blood Prince. *Harry Potter has just used the spell "Sectumsempra" against Draco Malfoy, and now Harry needs to hide the book from an angry Professor Snape. If you need further explanation, you're not a true Harry Potter fan so you can go ahead and skip this story because it's not for you.*

Harry ran through the halls, his heart racing. He needed to find somewhere to hide his book or he'd be expelled for sure.

He spotted a broom cupboard and opened the door.

Instead of a broom cupboard, though, Harry found himself in what appeared to be an entirely black room. It was perfectly square, like...a box. There was nothing on the walls except for a few bright posters and magically swirling gold words snaking around the room that read, YOU'RE ALWAYS AUDITIONING. At the foot of a raised platform sat approximately twenty students chanting a strange spell: "Black leather yellow leather black leather yellow leather."

"Er..." said Harry, wishing at once that he hadn't said anything, because everyone turned to him faster than you could diagnose Severus Snape with clinical depression.

"OH SNAP, IT'S HARRY FUCKING POTTER!" A girl wearing polka-dot robes ran up to him. "Are you here to audition?"

"Er..." said Harry again. "Er" really was his go-to phrase, he realized in that moment. Regaining his power to speak wordy words, he said, "Sorry, what...what is this place?"

"Welcome to the Hogwarts Drama Club!" all twenty voices said in unison.

"Hogwarts has a drama club?"

"Um, of course we do, talk to the hand!" said a boy in periwinkle robes. This phrase was not foreign to Harry, for they were living in the late nineties, something that strangely never came up in Harry's internal monologue.

"Ooooh, are you here to audition for *Carousel*?" said a girl wearing a T-shirt that magically flashed between a poster for something called *Our Town* and the words HDC MAINSTAGE 1995.

"Yes, we're in DESPERATE need of a baritone to play Billy Bigelow. Thomas over there can't seem to get the low notes."

"Guess it'll be my THIRD time playing Mr. Snow," said the boy called Thomas, following it up with a mediocre double pirouette. Everyone laughed. Harry didn't get the... joke?

The girl in polka-dot robes continued. "Well, this is quite the get for us. Harry, are you a baritone or a tenor?"

The last time Harry had been interrogated this much was when he talked to Rita Skeeter and he was not keen to repeat that experience. Wait a second, he realized. "Skeeter." That name sounded just like "mosquito." The fact she was a bug had been there that whole time? He laughed to himself. He really should pay more attention to the symbolism of people's names in this world.

The girl in polka-dot robes snapped him out of his reverie and repeated the question. "Are you a baritone or a tenor?"

Harry rolled his eyes. "Er...I really don't know. I'm just looking for a place to hide this book, and then I'll be on my way." He wished there were a spell to speed up awkward moments. That would be a lot more useful than turning spoons into badgers or whatever.

"We'll hide your book if you tell us what your vocal range is!"

Before Harry could protest, someone grabbed his hand, the Prince's book fell to the floor, and all the students were dragging him over to an upright piano in the corner of the room. As Harry approached, the piano opened up its top and wheezed, "What's this, another tone-deaf dud to be tested by ol' Ivory?" The sassy piano then played an excerpt from Mozart's Requiem. Everyone laughed again at the...joke?

Thomas chimed in. "No, Ivory, this is HARRY POTTER. He's the CHOSEN ONE. The one who defeated He-Who-Must-Not-Be-Named?"

"Well, let's hope this bloke is he-who-must-not-be-flat. All right, scruffy, let's see how you fare on some scales."

"Er..." The only scale Harry had ever heard of was the type a snake had. Were these students Parselmouths, like him? Were they practicing dark magic? Is that what made them all so goddamn annoying?

"Now, just go 'ahhh,'" said Ivory while playing notes that went up in a sequential order. Harry breathed a sigh of relief. If this is all it would take to hide his book, he'd been through worse!

"Ahhhhhh..." he began to sing.

The room was abuzz. Harry heard various mutterings of, "Baritone, definitely baritone," and "Could he BE any more of a bass?" in the style of Must See TV's mega-star, Chandler Bing.

Just as Harry was about to conjure up an excuse to leave, the door opened behind him. Harry whipped around, his heart racing. He drew out his wand, preparing to say "Expelliarmus" to whoever had just walked in because that continued to be the only defensive spell he could retain since, let's face it, Hermione was the real hero of this book series.

Harry was relieved to discover that it was not Professor Snape who had just walked in, but Professor Sinistra. Professor Sinistra was his astronomy teacher and, despite saying her name a few times in his inner monologue, he realized in that moment he'd never thought to properly describe her so any further description of her here is fair game.

"Now, what's going on here—" She saw Harry and froze. "Is that Harry Potter auditioning? Why, I haven't been this surprised since I landed the role of Helga on the wizard sitcom *Flying Blind*!"

The class burst into applause and Professor Sinistra waited for Harry to be impressed. When no change of facial expression came, she said, "I recurred on it during season two. I got to go to the HAG Awards that year."

Harry proffered an elegant, "Er..."

Her self-esteem wounded, Professor Sinistra changed the subject. "So you want to try out for *Carousel*, then? Are you a tenor or a baritone?"

Harry tried to protest and tell her that he was just there to hide his book, but the rest of the students ignored his clearly reluctant body language and drowned him out with differing replies.

"Okay, okay!" sighed Professor Sinistra. "Sometimes working with you children is as chaotic as a story in a certain hit wizarding workplace ensemble comedy." She drew her wand. "We'll let the casting hat sort this out. *Liza Minnellius!*"

She waved her wand and, all of a sudden, Harry felt something soft land on his head. The smell of whiskey and cigarette smoke filled the air and a female voice in an American accent slurred, "Oh boy, casting already? What a yummy tummy treat for this ol' hat today!" Harry realized that this must be a relative of the Sorting Hat, but one who specialized in casting plays. Reading his thoughts, the hat replied, "Quick thinking, Einstein! Now let Liza do her thing!"

The hat pressed tighter against his head and, Harry could swear, also pinched his ass. After a moment, she burped out, "Billy Bigelow! He's the lead, Billy Bigelow!"

The class was all atwitter. Harry saw this as his moment to pull a Cedric Diggory and exit unexpectedly. He dropped his book behind a ficus and started to back out of the room.

Polka-Dot Robes Girl put a hand on his shoulder. "Where are you going? You're the lead in the spring musical. It's time to start rehearsing!" She thrust a script into his hands as a magical tape measure appeared out of nowhere and started measuring his neck.

Harry felt claustrophobic as his personal space was invaded, an emotional trigger since he was forced to live in a cupboard for most of his life. Harry ignored his PTSD and sputtered, "I just came here to drop my book, I don't want any of this!" He turned to Thomas. "And Thomas, you deserve the lead! You've clearly earned it!"

Thomas shrugged. "When you have it, you have it. Can't argue with the hat."

The hat chimed in, "I was in *The Rink*!"

Harry sputtered some more. "B-b-but perhaps Professor Dumbledore could tell the hat to make an exception!"

The class laughed and Thomas said, "Uh, *that* bitch couldn't give less of a shit about the arts at this school. Next time you're palling around with that wannabe Gandalf to find Horcruxes or whatever, ask to take a peek at the yearly budget. I bet it's buried deep in the closet just like everything else."

Harry continued to sputter, "B-b-but you deserve the role so much more than I do!"

Thomas reassured him. "Don't worry about me, Harry, I've always suspected that acting wasn't my true calling and that I'd end up being a Floo Network executive."

As the class agreed with Thomas that yes, he was extremely

smart and they could definitely see him changing the culture of the Floo Network, Harry's mind raced. He was as confused as a Hufflepuff reading *The Sound and the Fury*. Harry had to get out of there and find a decoy potions book to show Snape. If only he had a distraction. And just then, it came to him. He had never done person-to-person transfiguration spells before, but desperate times...

He pointed his wand at one of the quieter students and said, "*Homenem Replaceo*." Instantly a perplexed middle-aged wizard in a gray suit stood in the student's place.

Professor Sinistra exclaimed, "Who are you? There's no Apparition allowed inside Hogwarts!"

The perplexed man in the suit stated, "My name is Gerald Smithwick, and I'm a West End casting director."

As soon as they heard the words "casting director," Professor Sinistra and the class swarmed poor Gerald. Liza Minnellius said, "Whaddya need, whaddya need? I'm willing to cut off my pointy tip and play a bonnet!" Amidst the commotion, Harry sneaked out of the room. Sighing with relief in the hallway, he slipped on his Invisibility Cloak as he tiptoed back to Gryffindor Tower. Man, he thought, this school sure was crazy sometimes!

EPILOGUE: NINETEEN YEARS LATER

Harry Potter stood with his little family in the queue outside the box office. Like the hundred or so other people standing with them, they, too, were desperate to score tickets for the West End production of *Hamilton*. It had been sold out online for months, but Harry was banking on the hope a witch or wizard might be working the box office and he could play the "I saved the world" card. Little Lily tugged on his sweater, squealing, "Daddy, when will we get the tickets? I'm DESPERATE to see the Schuyler Sisters' number in person!"

"It won't be long now, Lily," said a mildly frustrated Harry.

As he approached the window, he saw recognition dawn on the face of the old woman behind the glass. He was in. Harry smirked. This was gonna be easier than Ginny the night after the Battle of Hogwarts.

"Harry Potter?" said the old woman.

"Indeed, it is I. Listen, I know you're sold out, but if you don't mind making an exception for the Chosen One, we would LOVE five tickets for this Saturday—"

"Don't you remember me?" the old crone said.

"Er..."

"It's me. Professor Sinistra."

Harry couldn't believe his eyes. "You're working...here?"

"Yes. Shortly after Dumbledore died, the entire Hogwarts performing arts program was completely gutted. It's funny, the students all said that if you had stayed to play Billy Bigelow in *Carousel*, it might have been the boost that the drama department needed."

Harry didn't know what to say. "Right, sorry about that. So, erm, my tickets...?"

As Professor Sinistra slowly lowered the shade that said CLOSED, Harry knew the answer to his question. At long last, the drama club had had its revenge. Harry's scar burned for the first time in nineteen years. They would have to see *Mamma Mia!* instead. All was not well.

SOMEBODY STOP THEM! (FROM QUOTING JIM CARREY MOVIES)

Despite my experiences with bullies in my youth, I believe people to be fundamentally good at heart. Growing up has shown me that beneath any meanness there's a vulnerable, beautiful person who just doesn't know how to properly express their emotions.

Except for straight men in musical theater. Straight men in musical theater are irredeemable fuckfaces.

I'm sorry, that was harsh. What I mean to say is: 80 percent of straight men in musical theater are irredeemable fuckfaces. If you're a straight man in musical theater and this is offensive to you, feel free to tell yourself that you're part of that 20 percent fuckfaceless minority.

May I continue?

In such a highly personal book, you may wonder why I'm taking the time to rant about SMIMT (straight men in musical theater). The answer is: They annoy me. They annoy me when they try to overshadow me as an acting partner, they annoy me when they cheat on my friends they're dating, they annoy me when, after a hookup, they don't check to see if I've cum and then I'm inexplicably made to watch home videos of them and their parents playing mini golf. True story.

But the most annoying thing is that no one seems to call them out on their shit. So, ahem ahem, allow me. SMIMT: You are pompous yet cripplingly insecure. You hate yourselves while shit-talking anyone who threatens your dominance. You sing at altruistic nonprofit galas yet delight in making AIDS and dead baby jokes. Also, those jokes are from 2003 and you've hung on to them because the general low standard of humor in the musical theater community means you never had to actually get funny beyond a ninth-grade level. Indeed, your tendency to think of yourselves as "the funny guy" is one of the world's great tragedies. You conflate "humor" with quoting *Anchorman* or *Dumb and Dumber* and, even worse, you often have, shudder, a reel of celebrity impressions.

You'll notice that a lot of the above descriptors could apply to any straight man. But I'm calling you SMIMT out specifically because being in theater has tricked you into thinking you're not one of *those* guys. After all, you do theater! You're self-aware and empathetic! And hey, with your beautiful voices and ability to fake tears, most people would agree with you.

So why? Why do you suck shit? It all comes down to one thing: blowjobs.

See, SMIMT are both rare and highly coveted. Since many

of the great characters in musical theater, especially from the Golden Age of the 1950s through the 1970s, are straight and male (and largely white), there is a huge demand for the type of guy who can play these parts, and that "type" often aligns with actually being a self-identified straight cis man.[*] So when one of them is cast in a production, he is most likely surrounded by people who want to fuck him. This creates a feeding frenzy among the women in the cast and the musical theater community in general. Oh damn, he's talented AND he'd theoretically fuck me? Give me the gift of THAT grip-top sock!

Hence: the plentiful amounts of literal blowjobs that come to you early and easily. With all these blowjobs, you feel no need to better yourselves or question your terrible personalities. Blowjobs have stunted you. If it makes you feel better, it's not all your fault. *We* are part of the problem. We fall for your silky baritones and striking good looks: a Broadway 10, a Hollywood 5, and a Hedge Fund 3. And the few people who do fully clock your suckiness don't want to say anything because they don't "want to send Justin into one of his moods."

If you're reading this and are about to cast a straight man in your theater production, the most important tool you can arm yourself with is awareness. Here's a realistic casting breakdown of what you might be dealing with:

---

[*] To be clear: You don't need to be straight to *play* a straight man in a musical. But for whatever reason, the non-straight guys who get these roles tend to be way better people.

HAROLD HILL (*The Music Man*): 30s-40s. Baritone. The actor playing this role perceives himself to be "charismatic," and, unfortunately, so will most of the women in the show. He will hook up with every soprano in the cast (but never the altos, they're too threatening). He will eventually commit to the actress playing Marian, but they'll break up when she finds the actress playing Ethel Toffelmier licking his balls under the front desk of the library set after a Saturday matinee.

CURLY MCLAIN (*Oklahoma!*): 20s-30s. Baritone. He has landed the MOTHER lode of macho musical theater roles. Be prepared for rehearsal to run long so that he can "really get to know" his prop knife. He's gonna be really into that knife. It'll be weird how into the knife he is.

SWEENEY TODD (*Sweeney Todd*): 30s-50s. Bass–baritone. This guy thinks he's hot shit because he played baseball in high school. When he says "Hello," he really means, "You're welcome." He has also been assumed to be gay his whole life, so he thinks it gives him a free pass to do a "funny gay voice" when he feels insecure. He may even develop a *Mad TV*–like character around said funny gay voice. Get ready to hear a lot of, "Hiiiiii it's me, Bruuuuuuth! Who wants a QUICHE?" Enjoy tech week!

FIYERO (*Wicked*): 20s. Tenor. Thinks he can make any woman cum with just his dick. In a mediocre rock band.

FIYERO UNDERSTUDY (*Wicked*): 20s. Tenor. Knows how to make a woman cum. In a terrible rock band.

NICKY ARNSTEIN (*Funny Girl*): 30s-40s. Baritone. Move over, Brando, this guy went to SUNY Purchase! This actor in this role will naturally feel threatened by the woman playing Fanny so he'll find subtle ways to belittle her during rehearsal, like slowly clapping when she forgets a line or pointing out every time she has a period zit.

JIMMY SMITH (*Thoroughly Modern Millie*): 20s-30s. Tenor. Owns only one towel.

BILLY BIGELOW (*Carousel*): 20s-30s. Baritone. This guy is way too psyched for the scenes in which he gets to hit women. Gave the guy who played Jimmy Smith his towel because he had an extra one.

ALFRED DOOLITTLE (*My Fair Lady*): 50s-60s. Baritone. Has been in the game forever. The #MeToo movement makes him very nervous.

MY *PLAYBILL* BIO

RACHEL BLOOM (*Me*) still loves the world of theater very much despite the fact she has issues with it. Namely: every BFA musical theater program's emphasis on being a "triple threat" with little regard to the human being underneath, the Niles Crane-esque snobbery of the theater community, the general deification of "brilliant assholes," and the huge cover-up of a *New York Times* article that was going to be Broadway's own #MeToo reckoning. But Rachel acknowledges that her love of theater is a part of her that will never go away, nor does she want it to. In fact, the time she took away from doing theater gave her some perspective on it and put her back in touch with the child inside her that just wanted to sit and listen to the cast album of *Evening Primrose*. Recent credits of her still loving theater include: *Sobbing the First Time She Saw Hamilton*, *Watching*

Every Episode of Smash, Sobbing the Second Time She Saw Hamilton, Full-On Making a Musical Television Show, and *Always Sobbing at That One Part in Hamilton Where They All Sing "the Orphanage."* Love to her husband and Jesus...Christ Superstar.

PART 5:

NORMAL PEOPLE ARE SANE

AN APOLOGETIC ODE TO MY FORMER ROOMMATES

I had many unresolved issues with what I now understand to be depression and anxiety during my teens and early twenties. So when I run into people who knew me from ages eighteen to twenty-two, I feel a compulsion to say, "Hey, by the way, I had a lot of shit going on then," and then I give them a complete rundown of my therapy and medication history until they walk away. And there's one group of people around whom I feel a particular amount of cringiness...

Everyone has *that* roommate
You know, that one chick
The memory of whom
You can never unstick.
What made her so weird?
What the hell was she thinking?

You wonder with friends
When you're at a bar drinking.
When it comes to my case
Things are different, you see
For I'm sorry to say
That weird roommate was me.

To Riley and Angela
From freshman year
How did I show you thanks
For giving me my first beer?
With piles of clothes
Heaped onto my bed
Papers strewn on the floor
Homework, true, but unread.
Then there was that time
I took over the toilet.
My ass loudly exploded.
Your appetite, I did spoil it.
To be fair, I got food poisoning
From the Kosher dining hall
But my diarrhea was loud
And the room was too small.
Plus I'd cry all the time
My emotions were gory.
So to you both I say:
Wow I'm super sorry.

Let's move on to Fair Alex
In my sophomore year.
I learned nothing with age,
That much was clear.
I'd stay up until three
On AOL IM
And only shut my computer
When you'd cough, "AHEM."
I had horse blinders on.
Case in point as you'll see:
While you were still in the room
I took a dude's virginity.
Ooooof.

Then came the summer of Kristen
Or was it Kirsten? Don't care
'Cause you were a bitch.
But to be fair
I'd go on depressed walkabouts at 4:00 a.m.
Then come back in hacking up cigarette phlegm.
I'd fuck guys in the bathroom
While you were asleep
Then I'd cry every morning
From sadness so deep.
"Look at your life!"
You screamed at me that one night.

You lacked basic empathy
But, shit, you were right.

Victoria, please, forgive me
If you're able
For piling costumes
Over our kitchen table.
You had no room
For relaxing or reflecting
(Though, um, they *were* for a musical
I was directing).
But that's no excuse
For my manner so rude
And my dishes so dirty
With uneaten food
And old soap in the shower
That looked like cat vomit.
When you threw it out
And cleaned the residue with Comet
I was pissed at the time.
(That soap cost me five bucks!)
Yet now when I think of it
I'm just like "Fuuuuuuuuck."

To Michelle and Jeff:
I slept in so late
Which is why I regarded you

Both with such hate
When you'd make your smoothies
At eleven in the morning
I'd shout, "I'm still sleeping!"
Which, in retrospect, was annoying.
Though did you even care?
Maybe I get a pass?
Because most of the time
You both were high off your ass?

Regardless

No matter the year
No matter the season
I have no excuses
But I do have a reason.
See, I was a mess
Inside of my head
And that mess trickled out
To my bureau and bed.
I didn't figure my shit out
Till I moved in with my spouse.
Now I actually do dishes!
And tidy the house!
It took me a while
To get into the groove.
Therapy was key

And Prozac goes down so smooth.
Though, I'm still pretty messy
Yet there's never a quarrel.
How does my husband stand me?
Here is the moral:
To make a roommate okay
With your scattered wits
It helps when you let him
Cum on your tits.

MY HISTORY WITH
PLEASURE

I was born with an urge to seek out *pleasure*. I'm italicizing *pleasure* because if you could hear the way I say it, it just feels *italicized*. I once read an article about a sex toy maker in France who said that while sex is not taboo in American culture, *pleasure* is. Indeed, female *pleasure* is scary to some because you don't necessarily need a dick for it and the thought of a dick not being necessary at all times drives some folks cuckoo bananas. Although I don't claim to be the patriarchy's worst nightmare (straight lady married at twenty-seven and pregnant at thirty-two, super basic bitch), I am very proud to say that I valued sexual education and empowerment at such a young age that I actually learned how to masturbate from a book.

I had heard the word "orgasm" a few times throughout my childhood but had no idea what it meant. I only knew that it was a naughty word because every time it was uttered around me (usually in a TV show), my mother would gasp, look in my

141

direction, and then quickly change the channel. I repeatedly asked my parents what it meant, but they refused to tell me. When I was nine years old, we were at dinner with a family friend and, in talking about my parents' various rules that frustrated me, I blurted out, "AND they won't tell me what the 'o' word means!" The family friend looked at her confused husband and I saw her clarify by whispering, "Orgasm."

"Yes! That! What is it?" I demanded.

Off of my parents' "be my guest and take on this uncomfortable conversation" body language, their friend said, "It's...it's a feeling you get...after sex."

What? *That's* what the "o" word meant? What the fuck was the big deal?

It wasn't until I was reading a puberty book that I understood what the fuck *was* the big deal.[*] *What's Happening to Me?* told me a lot of things about my body I didn't know, but the part that blew my mind was the section about *masturbation*. It said that, to masturbate, boys will rub their penis and girls will "massage" their "clitoris," and the whole thing ends in an orgasm. I decided to try it out. You know, for science.

I'd never heard of this thing called a "clitoris" so I was happy that I found it instantly when spread-eagled on the floor looking

---

[*] I don't remember how this obsession with reading about my sexuality overlapped with my guilty thoughts (see: part 2), but I suspect I didn't feel as much guilt because my parents knew I had a bunch of puberty books so it didn't feel like something I was keeping from them.

into my bedroom's full-length mirror. Huh. Never noticed that before. It looked like the big nose of an old man.

It was time to get to work. Again, for science. I sat in my closet with the door closed. That way, in case anyone came in the room, I could say that I was "cleaning my closet" (which is actually a great masturbation euphemism). Not knowing what to expect, I gently touched myself through my underwear where the book said to. It instantly felt amazing and within five minutes, I understood what an "orgasm" was. My parents' friend was right: It was a big. Fucking. Deal. And with that, a new pastime rivaled theater for being my favorite thing to do ever.

By eighth grade, masturbating was my equivalent of a martini after work. I'd get home, take a shower, get in bed, flick the bean, fall asleep for three hours, wake up, eat dinner, and then study in front of the TV. Not content with this paltry amount of masturbation in my life, I got the brilliant idea in high school to masturbate WHILE studying. It was surprisingly effective; the night before my AP US history test, I masturbated on and off for three hours straight. On that test, I got a 4 (the second highest score) as well as a lifelong fetish for the Teapot Dome Scandal.*

When I started doing below-the-waist stuff with guys in college, I began to second-guess my own *pleasure* after a few people remarked that it took some "effort" to get me off. I

---

* That was one of my first stand-up jokes. I give it a B minus.

remember one guy going down on me for ten seconds and, when I didn't instantly cum, saying, "Wow, you're tricky." I got self-conscious. The scientific puberty books never told me that having to touch my clit for a long time made me "tricky." When I challenged guys on this, they'd tell me tales of "other girls" they'd been with who came from just penetration. In my mind, those "other girls" seemed pretty and easy and perfect. I imagined them all being named Stephanie.

I started to worry: Had masturbating at an early age "ruined" my ability to be a Stephanie? Discussing this with other women only made me feel worse because they either didn't want to talk about their bodies OR they readily bragged about how easily they came from just penetration. These were girls who said they never orgasmed until they were sexually active and, as a result, they hadn't "trained" themselves to need anything more than just a dick. When I'd reply that I just didn't think my body was built to cum from penetration, they would say I just needed to "relax," or maybe I just hadn't ever "really been in love." Fuck. Were these Stephanies right?

It took a podcast by a gay man to change the way I felt about my body. When I heard Dan Savage say on *The Savage Lovecast* that only about a quarter of women can achieve an orgasm through vaginal penetration alone, it validated me. I was RIGHT. Reading was once again my friend in my *pleasure* pursuit as I sought out every article I could find about the female orgasm. I learned that even vaginal orgasms most likely stem from the nerves of the clitoris, that the clitoris is infinitely more sensitive than the penis, and that an astonishing number of women fake orgasms (some of whom, I imagine, are named Stephanie).

By my late twenties, I was an out-and-proud clitoral cummer. I was proud of the way I achieved *pleasure*, how open I was at communicating what I needed to achieve *pleasure*, and how frequently I experienced *pleasure*.

And then I got pregnant.

Twist! The whole time I've been writing this book, I've also been gestating a child! I know! #Momspiration #Wombgoalz #Werkqween #Sunday. Despite the nausea and backaches and off-putting vaginal stench, I love being pregnant. I love feeling her kick, I love feeling her hiccup, and I love the fact she's with me all the time.

Except for when I masturbate.

When I masturbate, I pretend that she's somehow gone to a place far far away. Maybe to some sort of magical womb tree along with every other fetus whose mom is currently masturbating. They are safe in the tree, guarded by asexual fairies, until their moms cum, after which point the fetuses are free to reenter the womb.

Having a baby inside me just does not compute with *pleasure*. They are two different and disparate things. Yet, I don't feel this cognitive dissonance regarding sex during pregnancy. Sex, after all, is what makes babies in the first place. It's natural and beautiful and, during pregnancy, it's the only time in my

life I've ever been able to stomach the label "making love." *
But I don't extend the same sentimentality to when I'm gettin'
down to a Pornhub video called "Schoolgirl slut sucks cock
to get an A." I know that all the books say that the womb's
rhythmic contractions don't traumatize the fetus and actually
"lull them to sleep." But I dunno, what if this creates a bad
habit? What if, for the rest of her life, my future daughter
can only be soothed to sleep by the sound of someone gagging
on a dick screaming, "Oh baby yes yes yes I now love science
claaaaaaaass!"

So I have spent my life coming to terms with *pleasure*, but I
have still not come to terms with the original caveman reason
for it in the first place: reproduction. Of course, sex serves so
many purposes beyond that, but I can't get over that *pleasure* is
essentially Mother Nature's tricky sleight of hand. Like, what
a bitch. And if that weren't bad enough, the clitoris isn't even
essential to reproduction. We could theoretically still carry on
the species without a single woman cumming ever again.

Wait. That means that the clitoris only exists for one reason.
And that…is *pleasure (pleasure pleasure pleasure just imagine
that word echoing as it slowly fades away pleasure pleasure pleasure
pleasure pleasure).*

---

* Actually, I still can't. BARF.

MY STRICT RULES FOR WHIMSY

My likes and dislikes have not changed much since childhood. I am still obsessed with amusement parks, musicals, large reptiles, and the eerie similarities between the Lincoln and Kennedy assassinations (John Wilkes Booth ran from a theater and was caught in a warehouse! Lee Harvey Oswald ran from a warehouse and was caught in a theater!). A word you could use to describe me is "whimsical." But whimsy has always been a serious business for me. Being the kid who didn't want anyone's parents coming backstage before the school play because it would "break the fourth wall," I have certain rules for fun by which I abide and expect others to do the same. For some, it's off-putting and intense. For others, it's also off-putting and intense.

The below list of rules has taken me thirty-three years to curate. Half of it is Disney-related.

1. The correct amount of being into Disneyland is the exact same amount that I am into Disneyland. If you are into Disneyland less than I am then you are an unimaginative cynic. If you are into Disneyland any more than I am, it's like, I DON'T CARE ABOUT YOUR PIN COLLECTION, FREAK.

2. When entering a Disney park, you may debate Walt Disney's rumored anti-Semitism. However, you may ONLY do it when walking down Main Street.

3. The actors in the Harry Potter movie series are NOT the actual characters. They are actors playing the characters in the Harry Potter books, all of whom are real, and I will meet them someday.

4. When greeting my dog, do not say, "Hey buddy!" She is not a "buddy." She is a princess, stinker, sock monster, Madam, Peanut Wolf, pillow, fly assassin, and maybe "special friend." But not "buddy."

5. Back to Disneyland: If someone in your party gets sick on a ride, then it is perfectly acceptable to abandon that person in the nurse's station and continue on with your day. I have done this to my husband on three separate occasions and feel no guilt.

6. And while we're on the subject: When on the Disneyland ride Indiana Jones and the Temple of the Forbidden Eye, do NOT look into the eyes of the stone goddess Mara. I mean, I shouldn't have to say this because the warning is right in the ride title, but, inevitably, someone in your car

will look. Yes, this violation is the catalyst for the entire ride, but show some cultural respect. You do not need to be part of the problem.

7. When skipping through a field of flowers and giggling, closed-toe shoes must be worn.

8. In the game "Never Have I Ever," please stick to sex- and drug-related activities. No one wants to know who in the group hasn't seen *Citizen Kane*.

9. Back to Disneyland again. The entirety of Splash Mountain / parts of Small World / half of the Jungle Cruise is racist. I have no idea what to do about it, but it does need to be verbally acknowledged at some point on each ride. The discussion around this cognitive dissonance must last twice as long if everyone in your party is white.[*]

10. If English is your native language and you always mix up "their" and "they're," then YOU ARE NOT A RAVEN-CLAW.

11. If I'm showing you one of my many childhood home movies (again, there are seventy-two of them), please do not comment on the action until I press PAUSE.

12. Every name for an iguana is fair game except "Connor."

13. Blair Witch still rules.

---

[*] As of May 2020 it looks like some of this is actually changing. Better eighty years late than never I guess, House of Mouse!

JAFAR AND THE WET BANDITS

In 2010, it had been years since I'd encountered the "Guilty Itch," "The Bad," "OCD," whatever you want to call the thing from part 2, pick your favorite name. Sure, I had some other problems (see: the roommate poem), but since I wasn't experiencing repetitively guilty thoughts, I rarely thought about that period in my life at all. The memories were too painful and why dwell on the past because I was all better now. Case closed, gavel once again goes bang bang! Thinking the bad times were behind me, I launched into my twenties with all the hubris of the hero at the start of a movie sequel. Jafar would NEVER come back because I, Aladdin, had banished him to live in a magic lamp in the previous movie! The Wet Bandits would NEVER come back because I, Kevin McCallister, had banished them to jail in the previous movie! And my obsessive thoughts would never come back because I, Rachel Bloom, had banished them to the distant fog of memory in the previous movie! And also I had pierced ears and was fucking now so I was clearly a very different person!

But of course the villain came back. Had this part of my life been a movie sequel, the critics would have called it, "An unsurprising and obvious installment in the series."

When my boyfriend Gregor* told me in 2009 that he was moving from New York to LA, I was upset but not surprised. It was, after all, the basic bitch New York comedian thing to do at that time, so I had assumed this was happening sooner or later. I couldn't yet justify moving back to LA for my own career, so until I figured out my shit, Gregor and I would be in a...Long-Distance Relationship. Ugh. The only phrase in the English language worse than "Long-Distance Relationship" is "I'm calling about your lab results. Do you have time to talk?"

After I drove cross-country with Gregor, he dropped me off at LAX for my flight back to New York. As we kissed good-bye, my mind was flooded with questions about the unknown. Could our relationship survive with us being three thousand miles apart? What if he met someone else hotter, smarter, more sophisticated? What if he finally realized that I was too dorky and lame for him? He was so cool and experienced; how many women had he slept with anyway?

Huh. That last question was...kind of a non sequitur. Weird move, brain. I tried to shake it free. But it stuck with me. I

---

* Colonel Pennyfeather. There.

fixated on this random-ass question during my walk through the airport, on the plane, and on the cab ride back to my apartment. How. Many. Women. Had. Gregor. Slept. With. Why the fuck couldn't I stop thinking about this inconsequential question? Why did I care about Gregor's sexual history? Stop it! Stop thinking about this question, brain! You're doing this to yourself, you stupid bitch!*

When three days went by and I still had this weird fixation, I thought: Wait a second. Mulling over an irrational question, feeling nothing but dread, and then feeling compelled to repeat the cycle over and over again?

Oh fuck. Jafar was back. And this time...he brought the Wet Bandits.**

No no no, I told myself. The thing that happened to me in middle school couldn't be happening to me again. Yet I had all the signs: the intrusive questions, the constant dread, even the stomachaches. Why, why, why was this happening again? I blamed myself. I was voluntarily doing this. I was *willing* The Bad back into existence because I was *weak*. And as I beat myself up, The Bad mutated. My intrusive thoughts became centered on the thoughts themselves. Like: How long would The Bad last this time? What if The Bad was here to stay? What if The Bad suddenly colored how I felt about my boyfriend and now every time I thought about my boyfriend I also

---

*   Ooh ooh Easter Egg ooh ooh!
**   Which would have been a better plot for *The Return of Jafar*.

thought about The Bad? The repetitive thoughts continued because, if I thought about my thoughts long enough, I could "solve" The Bad. If I could figure out the reason it had come back, I might crack the code and it would go away.

Critics would have said about *this* part of the sequel: "The second act is convoluted and boring. I went to get popcorn and when I came back, I had missed nothing. Two thumbs down."

In the middle of this, a music video I put online went, as the kids say, viral. Within weeks, I flew out to LA to meet with representation and within a few months I had agents, my first professional writing job, and a reason to move out and be with Gregor. I was so distracted by all these new developments, I didn't have space in my brain for the intrusive thoughts. One day, I woke up and I didn't feel The Bad anymore. It was just…gone. I was triumphant. I knew it would end! Jafar was finally dead! The Wet Bandits were denied parole! And I was free.

But a few months later, The Bad came back. For the next five years, this cycle repeated. There were more sequels of The Bad than in the *Land Before Time* series. It would always happen like this:

Step 1: A random but troubling question would appear in my brain.
Step 2: I would try to analyze why this question was there in the first place.

Step 3: I would analyze the analysis of the question.

Step 4: Oh shit, The Bad is back. This means all of these questions are going to consume me whole until The Bad taints everything I hold dear.

Step 5: What was the original question again?

Step 6: Get distracted with some new job/creative project/ good plate of pasta.

Step 7: Back to Step 1 four to six months later.

Then in May 2013, I received an email that would change my life forever: the screenwriter Aline Brosh McKenna had seen my music videos and wanted to discuss doing a potential musical TV show with me. Within ten minutes of us meeting, Aline pitched me the idea of *Crazy Ex-Girlfriend*, I went nuts for it, and we were off to the races. In what seemed like seconds, she and I had a full pitch for a television show.

I couldn't contain my excitement the night before the first round of pitches. This was it. It was all happening for me. All I had to do now was not fuck up the pitch, and—Oh shit, it's already 12:30 a.m.?!

I put my head down on the pillow to go to sleep. Nothing happened. As minutes passed and I still wasn't asleep, I panicked. "Oh God. What if I don't sleep so I'm too tired tomorrow and I fuck up the pitch and it ruins my life?" You would be right in remarking that I took it from A to C real quick.

And just like the night before fourth grade, I didn't sleep

at all the night before the *Crazy Ex-Girlfriend* pitches. When I met up with Aline the next day, I looked like I had been hit by a truck. When I told her that I didn't get any sleep the night before, she said, "Oh, honey, that's just nerves, you're gonna be great!" Not knowing me well then, she thought it was just "nerves." If only. I longed for the "nerves" that normal people felt.

But Aline was right. I DID do great in the pitches because adrenaline pushed me through the fatigue. But this didn't help me feel better. Delirious from the lack of sleep the previous night, I feared what would happen if I, once again, couldn't sleep. That night, the fear of not sleeping kept me from sleeping. Panicked, I took a Benadryl, and when that didn't work, I contacted a twenty-four-hour house-call doctor I found on Yelp to prescribe me a single sleeping pill. I'd never taken sleeping pills before, but I was desperate. I drove to the pharmacy, picked up my single sleeping pill, and then, chickening out, cut it in half. After all, what if the sleeping pill made me addicted? That's how sleeping pills work, right?

With some Benadryl and half a sleeping pill in my system, I still *couldn't sleep*. At 6:00 a.m., I called my friend Dan in a panic. Dan was a doctor doing his residency on the East Coast, so I knew he'd be up. I sobbed to him on the phone: What's wrong with me? Why am I broken? Whatever The Bad was, it had combined with insomnia to form a superstorm of depression and dread and panic. It was like this movie franchise had really gone off the rails and Jafar had fucked the Wet Bandits and it had also been a threesome with Voldemort and the baby that resulted from it was me.

After Dan talked me down a bit he told me to get back into my real bed; I'd been sleeping on a mattress on the floor of the office so as not to wake Gregor with my insomnia. When I got into bed with Gregor and he saw the state I was in, he said to not worry about sleep, just try to rest. Those were the first words of comfort I'd heard in days. Taking away the pressure to sleep was the only way I finally fell asleep. It was only for three hours, but it was something.

The next night I didn't want to risk anything, so I called that house doctor, got another sleeping pill, and this time, I took the whole thing. Fuck it. I'd become an addict.

But when I woke up, I wasn't an addict. Instead I'd slept nine hours and felt back to my old self. Glad that was over and never to return!

…Until a few days later when I had to get up the next morning for another early meeting. Once again, I dreaded the night and the horrors it could bring. It had become muscle memory at this point.*

---

* I should say that this whole time I was in therapy but my therapist wasn't…great, because when I described my anxiety she just said, "Hmm, you're very complicated." Cool. Thanks, lady! The best therapist I had during this time was actually my voice teacher. He was a chill opera singer from the South who said, "My mama always compared bad thoughts to a bird in a barn. If a bird flies into the barn, you can acknowledge that there's a bird in the barn, but you don't have to suddenly make a nest for it. Just let the bird fly in and it'll eventually fly out." Which is, in essence, cognitive behavioral therapy.

When I went back to New York for a friend's wedding that December, the jet lag made my sleep anxiety even worse, and eventually this turned into a dread that haunted me all day. I had never felt worse. And then, in the middle of this, Gregor got down on one knee in front of his old West Village apartment and proposed.

Part of me was the happiest I'd ever been in my life. But the other part of me was still feeling The Dread. (That's a new name for The Bad, catch up.) I was fed up and frustrated and furious at myself. Why did I continue to ruin my own life by thinking these thoughts? On the outside I was smiling and rapping "Baby Got Back" at the surprise karaoke party thrown by our friends, but on the inside, I was screaming at myself, *This is the best night of your life! Don't feel dread! Don't be an anxious cunt! Be! Happy!*

When I got back to LA, I was in very bad shape. I now felt a constant sense of overwhelming depression and I couldn't stop thinking my circular thoughts and I couldn't solve them and nothing would make them go away. I was nauseous all the time. My hormones were out of control. I couldn't concentrate. And I knew that I was doing this to myself. I was letting The Dread ruin my life.

And then something amazing happened.

I booked a T-Mobile commercial. STAY WITH ME HERE.

Knowing that my call time for the T-Mobile commercial was 6:00 a.m. the next day, I lay in bed as usual, nervous about being unable to sleep for a high-stakes morning event, as usual, all of the questions roaring in my ear, as usual.

And then another question entered my head. This wasn't in the sinister voice of the other questions. It wasn't The Dread. This question had a softer, kinder tone and it said, "Hey, you DO realize you're getting this worked up over a *T-Mobile commercial*?"

Oh GOD. That question was right. What the fuck was I doing? I didn't care about T-Mobile. I wasn't even a T-Mobile customer. I was with AT&T. Now, THAT would be a commercial to freak out about.

I grabbed my computer, went on *Psychology Today*'s therapy finder website, and sought out, for the first time, a psychiatrist. And when I walked into his office two days later, I told him EVERYTHING. I told him about the bad thoughts I'd had at age nine, how they transformed into all these catastrophic relationship and career fears, how it felt like The Bad was always coming for me to destroy everything I held dear. I barfed out everything I'd been ashamed to admit to myself for the past twenty-six years. And at the end of the barfing, I said to him ten words I'd never said before: "I want to change and I need help doing so." And I meant "help" in every sense: help with fighting the intrusive thoughts, help with changing my perspective on life, and, most important, chemical help.

I took a deep breath and prepared myself for his diagnosis of whatever weird thing was happening to me. But instead, he told me that what I was experiencing was stuff he'd seen before.

The specific diagnosis didn't matter; all I needed to know was that I wasn't a freak and I certainly wasn't "voluntarily doing this to myself."

Rather than naming a specific *illness* that I needed to treat, my doctor preferred to approach the whole thing from a more holistic level. My intrusive thoughts, my ups and downs with romantic obsession, and the feelings of misery I'd had throughout my life (see again: the roommate poem) were all connected. Under his guidance, I learned so many things over the next six months. I learned how to meditate to help me stay in the present. I learned how to sort out which thoughts were important to dwell on and which thoughts were trying to trick me. I learned the beauty of a pill called Prozac.

And I learned that The Bad, The Dread, The Hungry Hungry Manson Caterpillar—again, pick whatever name you like—will never really go away. It will always be a part of me. Even now, during high-pressure moments, an irrational question or feeling of dread will sometimes pop up like a tiny little Jafar tapping me on the shoulder. And when that happens, I try not to blame myself or solve the problem or fear that it's happening. I try to just...let it be. Does that always work? No. Because this shit is fucking hard.

However, I'd like to think that if my life were indeed a movie, a critic would say of this part: "A satisfying end to a confusing but ultimately rewarding franchise."

PART 6:

NORMAL PEOPLE CHOOSE SAFE CAREERS

MY LINKEDIN PROFILE CIRCA 2010

Rachel Bloom
Specialist in Literally Whatever Will Pay the Bills I
Truly Don't Care
New York, NY

Experience
Singing Waitress on a Boat
The Spirit of New York and *The Spirit of New Jersey* Dinner
Cruises
January 2010–October 2010

I was a waiter that sang songs on a three-hour cruise around
Manhattan for an audience unaware that they opted into a
cruise with singing waiters. When the songs came on a few
in the crowd would cheer; some would politely watch; and
many averted their eyes. In addition to my signature song "I'm
So Excited," I was also proficient in the nautical-themed song

parody of "I Got a Feelin'" (sample lyric: "Tonight's the night / Take off your coat / And rock the boat"). When someone ordered a gin and tonic, I knew how to upsell by saying, "Okay, so a Tanqueray and tonic, got it," then running away before they could clarify that they didn't want top-shelf liquor.

Reservationist
A NYC Fine Dining Restaurant
May 2009–December 2009

I sat at the entryway of the restaurant to "handle the reservations" but was really there to turn away any man attempting to walk in the restaurant wearing a tank top. When Hasidic Jews would come in for dates on the terrace, I was instructed to charge them (and only them) a $20 cover since "those people only ever order sodas." I graciously smiled when Italian tourists would yell at me and when the owner would remark how small my nose was for a Jewish girl. Also, I was very chill that one time when I was instructed to get in the car of the owner, was driven by the owner to an unknown location, and waited with the car idling in the red zone when he went to a party. Bonus skill: distracting the health inspector while someone closed the doors that led to a secret and unpermitted second kitchen.

Telemarketer for Nonprofit Theaters
Some call center, the name of which I've blocked out of my memory because it was a very sad place

January 2009–May 2009

I called people who saw *The Nutcracker* at the Pittsburgh Ballet Theatre once in 1996 to ask if they were interested in purchasing a full subscription that year. The one instance in which someone was actually interested, I talked her out of the sale because she revealed she was broke and her daughter had cancer. Other job duty: patiently listening to boss while he explained this job wasn't his true passion and promising to watch YouTube videos of his cabaret act.

Chocolate Seller
Max Brenner Union Square
November 2008–January 2009

Worked over the holidays at this popular chocolate shop and restaurant. One time in the storeroom, a co-worker said that if he couldn't make a woman cum with "just his dick" he didn't feel like a man. Have no idea how the conversation segued from chocolate to that.

Fundraising Caller
NYU Phonathon
January 2007–December 2007

The main fundraising program for NYU. I called alumni to ask them to give the school money with the justification that the "Princeton Review rates schools partially based on alumni satisfaction and the way that's recorded is through donations from alumni like you!" I took a long, hard look at myself in the mirror when one caller said, "Sweetie, you and I are both smart women and you know that's not true."

Camp Counselor
Prestigious Arts Summer Camp
Summer 2006

Fellow counselors were not teenagers, but full-grown adults. The job paid $800 for the entire summer. What adults would accept this paltry amount of money? Weird ones. In addition to my duties of overseeing camp activities, I would take it in stride when my colleagues would talk nonstop about Jesus and when one said the Bible would call me a "false Jew." I also played along when another counselor pretended to be deaf around the kids for a "social experiment" that was approved by the camp administration. Was honestly a pretty fun summer, though.

Education
New York University
Bachelor's Degree in Nothing Relevant to These Jobs Let's Move On

Skills
Smiling
Coercing
Not seeming hungover at eight in the morning

Balancing five cheesecakes on my arms while fighting my
way through a crowd dancing "Cupid Shuffle"
Again, nothing I went to school for

Recommendations

"Hi, I'm the guy from that camp story who pretended to be
deaf. You're probably wondering what that was all about so I'll
tell you. Basically, when all of us counselors got to camp, I was
introduced to everyone as a 'deaf person' who could read lips
perfectly. People would speak to me and then I would answer
back in, well, a 'deaf voice.' Then, the day before camp started,
I gathered all of the counselors in a room and said in my real
voice, 'Yeah guys, I'm not really deaf.' Everyone was shocked.
See, I was doing a college paper about how society treats the
deaf and I was going to compare the way the counselors treated
me before and after they knew my secret. Part of the paper was
about how children treat the deaf, so I got clearance from the
camp administration to pretend to be deaf the whole summer.
Toward the end, I got tired of the whole charade and would go
in and out of the 'deaf voice,' which many of the kids noted.
It was weird for everyone involved. Oh and I guess Rachel was
fine at the job, I'm not sure, I was pretty distracted by the fake
deaf thing." —Guy Who Pretended to Be Deaf

I'D LIKE TO DEDICATE THIS AWARD TO...

Wow, wow, wow. Thank you so much for this award. It means so much to me. And, hot take: It's heavy! Well there are so many people I need to thank, but there's one that really stands out. No, not God, LOL. I'm talking about Rejection.

No, really, I mean it. I want to thank Rejection. I know a lot of people *say* that they're grateful for Rejection but it's really just them reverse-engineering their failures to fit some sort of "meant-to-be" narrative. Honestly, though: Rejection really helped me. And I'm so grateful that so many different types of Rejection are here to support me in the audience tonight. I have to say, you all don't look a day over Eternal.

Let's start with Romantic Rejection. Can we get a camera on Romantic Rejection? That's right, it's the little baby cupid in the corner crying blood. There he is! And he's wearing a teeny-tiny tux! Aww.

As you'll recall, Blood Cupid, I was in a bad place in 2008.

It was summer vacation and I was reeling from a breakup.[*] Back at my parents' house, I decided to comfort re-read one of my favorite books, Ray Bradbury's *The Martian Chronicles*. I had always marveled at how Bradbury managed to use high-concept ideas to explore emotionally complex characters. This time, re-reading his work made me think about how my ex-boyfriend (who had become more emotionally distant than a calculator wearing khakis and a Kmart performance fleece) was the opposite of Ray Bradbury. I thought, wow—Ray Bradbury is the perfect man: intelligent in both mind and heart. If only I could find someone like him. Tickled by that idea, I sat at my parents' piano and wrote the first draft of a song called "Fuck Me, Ray Bradbury." More on that later, Blood Cupid.

Which brings me to my second rejection. It's that entire group of people sitting at the table in the front row, wearing tuxes, also crying blood. You are, of course, the rotating powers that be at the Upright Citizens Brigade Theatre. For years I took your classes, longing for nothing more than to make it onto one of your coveted house improv or sketch teams. And that never happened. Yet even though I was rejected from literally every team the theater could throw at me (sometimes it felt like teams were invented just so I could be rejected from them), I didn't want to give up on performing there.

So I started to write my own sketch show. Part of this new show was a silly song about the movie *Space Jam*. I had taken

---

[*]   Courtesy of the Earl of Laffland.

170

a musical theater writing class before but this was the first time I thought that maybe I could combine my musical theater background with sketch. When I played the demo for my boyfriend, expecting him to politely chuckle, he paused the demo. "Wait a sec, Rach. No one is doing shit like this. Why don't you make the whole sketch show a musical thing?" And that's how I started focusing on musical comedy.

I'm being played off but wait, I have to get to my final rejecter! Wearing that lovely Carolina Herrera gown and, of course, also crying blood, is my first "manager," Susan. Susan, dear, you'll notice that I have put the word "manager" in quotes because I later learned that anyone can in fact call themselves a manager, no credentials needed! This shed some light on your professionalism and why, after seeing me in a friend's internet sketch at age twenty-three, you became convinced that I could pass for sixteen and become a sexy teen star. "You're gonna get me my beach house," you'd say as you chain-smoked and "told me all about the industry" and how you and CAA were taking a "mutual break." I had never fancied myself a sexy teen star. "I do musical theater and comedy," I said, but you told me that you had a "gut feeling" and had me fly out to LA to audition for a CW teen sci-fi pilot about sexy shapeshifters. When the feedback from the casting director wasn't good, you instantly dropped me as a client and I never heard from you again.

Susan, I gotta say, I was really upset at the time. I wanted you back, baby. I realized that I needed to make something that would show you that I *was* special, that I *could* be a sexy teen star. And that's how I got the idea to turn that random song, "Fuck Me, Ray Bradbury," into a music video.

I was surprised that I didn't hear from you, Susan, when "Fuck Me, Ray Bradbury" took off online. Maybe you were busy with another budding teen star. Or maybe you finally got emphysema. In either case, that video's success landed me real representation (though none of them had the confidence in me to say I was going to get them their beach house).

So thank you, Rejection, for existing. For the record, I never saw you as an unjust force hell-bent on fucking me over. My breakup was the logical conclusion to an unsustainable relationship; my improv and sketch writing skills needed more polishing and it took me years to learn how to audition well. Facing you forced me to get better and pushed my life in all sorts of new directions. Ultimately, you triggered my fear of my mortality; the fear of being on my deathbed and realizing my life had meant nothing. You also triggered the feeling of spite. And, as I always say, when the fear of death falls in love with spite, the two of them make a beautiful baby named ambition. I actually just made that up right now, but I'll be sure to always say it from here on out.

Anyway, thank you! And thank you to HBO and my amazing co-stars Meryl Streep, Paul Lynde, and Richard Burton!

SAMPLE RÉSUMÉ!

So you want to be an actor! Well, first, you're gonna need a résumé. Since I'm sure you found that my LinkedIn profile was a useful template for your own career, I've included a résumé template below. Follow my guide, and before you know it, Hollywood / Broadway / Vancouver Because That's Where the Production Tax Breaks Are will be banging down your door!

LEARY O'MEGAN

(original name: Megan O'Leary)

(Name given to me by the male co-workers at my restaurant job: SugarPrincess)

Hair: Whatever color you want it to be, unless you want me bald, that's cool too

Weight: None of your business LOL; 100 pounds

Height: 5'3"

Height on stilts: 6'5"

Height when curled up into a ball crying on the phone to my parents begging them for rent money this month: 2'4"

Height when being harassed at my restaurant job: Disappear into floor

REGIONAL THEATER CREDITS

The Seagull	U.S. Arkadina; took over role when original actress was sadly blackmailed into dropping out	National Academy of Talent
The Vagina Monologues, The Musical	Singing Vagina	National Academy of Talent (Blackbox)
Annie *(Note: Is a different musical called Annie but was still based on the character from the "Little Orphan Annie" cartoon)*	Grace Farrell	Pisswater Falls Summer Stock (Note: Production never opened due to lawsuit)
Oklahoma!	"Oklahoma" (title character)	Twin Palms Teen Playhouse
Grease	Sandy #5 (show was quintuple cast)	Twin Palms Children's Players
Oliver!	Mrs. Bumble	Living room of a house once owned by the actress Hedy Lamarr

FILM/TV/INTERNET CREDITS

Shark Tank	Surfboard model for presentation of the invention "Surf-And-Turf-Board" (surfboard that also cooks food with wavepower energy)	No Deal
Pussy Juice Vaginal Lubricant (commercial)	Lady with Dry Pussy	Featured on Bangyoulater.com

TRAINING

Voice:	Emmeline's School of Singing/Bartending
Acting for Film:	Studied the "Be Famous Now!!" acting technique under Jared Prinz (godson of Hedy Lamarr)
Theater Training:	National Academy of Talent (Acting, Singing, Ballet, Doing all 3 with a raging hangover; Minor in the Study of Edgy Revivals)

Special skills: Voice, acting, ballet, tap, can fake a seizure, dialects (Russian, Yugoslavian, Estonian, Romanian), egg donation, blackmail

GENTLEMEN, MAY I KILL YOUR BONERS?

I was skeptical when I started getting invited to parties in high school. Me? A social gathering? Is this another prank? Is that fucker Devon McElroy hiding behind that couch?

Now, granted, these first parties were thrown by other drama kids, but they were *older* drama kids who did cool stuff like smoke cloves and play improv drinking games. My mind was really blown when I started partying with people who *weren't even in theater*. As I shared bottles of Mike's Hard Lemonade with the rebels from Marching Band or Yearbook or Model UN (my standards were low), I wondered: What about me had changed to warrant this drastic social upgrade? I made a list.

1. Doing drama was slightly cooler in high school.
2. I stopped cutting my own hair.
3. I upped my fashion game by maybe 5 percent.

4. I got contacts.

5. And, of course, tits.

And that was it. Those five things represented the line between misery and acceptance.

Which was fucking *ridiculous*. *This* is what had kept me from social acceptance for years? Some surface-y shit?

I was an abnormal person who could now "pass" as normal and I felt like a spy. I observed those around me, taking notes to send back to my mother country of Freakadonia,* and saw so many inherent contradictions in how people were expected to be versus how they actually felt on the inside. I saw this tension every time someone pretended not to be bothered by a "joking" insult, every time people pretended to love shitty dance music, every time someone had a quarter of a beer and was "so fucking wasted, bro."

By the time I got to college, I was fascinated by all of the contrasts between how we're told life is supposed to be and how it really is. I liked to think about the dark and the light, the resilient and the vulnerable, the gross and the beautiful, and how dangerously close these things were to each other. And nowhere was the contrast more inherent than in sex. I'd spent a lifetime fantasizing about when I'd start hooking up, and when it finally happened I found it fun, sure, but also awkward and smelly and pinch-ey and wet. This thing that I'd built up

---

*   Formerly part of the USSR.

in my mind for so long as a "normal" rite of passage also had all these unspoken gross human things. Breasts were floppy, penises were ugly, vaginas were stinky and balls were even stinkier. Jesus Christ, were they STINKIER.

So I was so happy to find out that romantic love could also be taken down from its ethereal pedestal. After one of my heartbreaks I desperately Googled one night, "How to fall out of love???" When I saw article after article about the science behind love and infatuation, I realized that love, too, had a gross and mundane side. This thing that had caused me so much agony wasn't so special after all. Love wasn't a "many-splendored thing"—it was actually a psychological term called "limerence." (I really should have been paying attention to the witch all those years ago.) Limerence, I read, was influenced by brain chemistry, our self-esteem, how much someone reminded us of our parents, armpit smell, and many other cringe-y things that were a far cry from any song by Rodgers and Hammerstein. (Some more realistic titles of theirs would be, "People Will Say We're in Limerence," "If I Loved You...I Would Remind Myself That It Would Be Influenced by Many Factors," and "Some Enchanted Evening We'll Go to Couples Therapy.")

All of this influenced my aforementioned first music video, "Fuck Me, Ray Bradbury," in which I wanted to explore the contrast between how the world appeared and how it actually was. In this case, it was what pop music called sexy versus what I called sexy. Yet when I read the YouTube comments (obvious tip: Never read YouTube comments), I was annoyed when people said that I looked "hot" in the video. (I mean, let's be honest, I was also psyched. But for the purposes of this story, let's say that I was only annoyed.) I was annoyed because looking hot wasn't the fucking point. I only looked "hot" because people looked hot in the music videos I was satirizing. I didn't want to "pass" as normal anymore—I wanted to make fun of it the way normal people had made fun of me.

I worried that if people were watching the video in an unironic sexy way, what if someone unironically jerked off to it? What if some guy got *pleasure* from the very thing I was trying to lampoon? So in every sexy song I ever did moving forward, I made sure to put in a boner-killer moment. A moment that, if you were jerking off to this video, you'd go soft. Ooooooh, you like my tits, big boy? Yeah, you like when I shake them? THEN HERE'S A PICTURE OF A ROTTING CAT CARCASS.* I wanted to remind the world that, even though I could pass as normal, I still wasn't. Because, well, nothing was.

When I stepped onto the set of "The Sexy Getting Ready Song" during the pilot of *Crazy Ex-Girlfriend*, it was a dream come true: Finally, one of my song ideas had actual money behind it. It looked like a real music video with chandeliers, a waterfall; we even hired one of Beyoncé's backup dancers

---

* Examples of boner-killer moments in my earlier YouTube work: Golda Meir's scolding in "You Can Touch My Boobies," the vomiting in "Jazz Fever," and the aborted fetus in "Die When I'm Young."

from the "Single Ladies" video. I felt like a real, unironic pop star.

Until I pretended to wax my asshole and blood splattered everywhere. As I watched the mostly male crew look away in disgust, I imagined any boners they may have had climbing up inside their bodies. It made me smile.

PART 7:

NORMAL PEOPLE DON'T GET BULLIED . . . AGAIN

EXTRA! EXTRA! HISTORY REPEATS ITSELF!

Thirteen-year-old Rachel: Hi Rachel! Thank you so much for sitting down with me today. I've been secretly writing newspaper articles in Microsoft Word's two-column format about my future imagined self for a while now, but this is the first time I've actually gotten my REAL future self to sit down for an interview!

Twenty-three-year-old Rachel: Yeah, it's so amazing that I happened to go to a time travel neuron chamber at the exact moment you happened to be sitting on one of earth's strongest electromagnetic energy pockets!

Thirteen-year-old Rachel: Let's not go too deep into the scientific logic of how this interview happened, otherwise we'll be here all day!

Twenty-three-year-old Rachel: Totally. In fact, our readers probably have way more questions now that we've semi-explained how this works as opposed to if we'd just presented the premise at face value!

Thirteen-year-old Rachel: Yep! So, I am interviewing myself exactly ten years from now! It's 2010! What's your/our life like?

Twenty-three-year-old Rachel: Um, not to brag, but my life is pretty amazing. Long story short, I released a comedic music video on the internet which got me managers and an agent and now I have my first professional comedy writing job!

Thirteen-year-old Rachel: Wow. Okay. This is a lot to take in!

Twenty-three-year-old Rachel: The bottom line is: You're happy.

Thirteen-year-old Rachel: Wow, sounds like things have really changed since middle school. Tell me...what's your average day like?

Twenty-three-year-old Rachel: Well, I wake up, kiss my awesome boyfriend goodbye as he goes to work, walk the dog, and then get to the office around ten. The job is a little intimidating—I'm the youngest person on the writing staff, the only woman, and I definitely have the least experience out of everyone there. But the bosses are nice and I'm surrounded by SUCH funny guys. Seriously, they're SO funny. A few of them are SO funny that I often can't even get a word in!

Thirteen-year-old Rachel: That's kind of annoying, right?

Twenty-three-year-old Rachel: Nah, little girl, it's not annoying, it's called being in a PROFESSIONAL WRITERS' ROOM. I'm the lowest on the totem pole so it's my job to suck up some humiliation here and there. Like, sometimes when I pitch a joke it falls flat (because, again, I'm new at this), but then someone else will make a joke about how bad my joke was and everyone laughs at THAT joke. Man, I'm so grateful to have this job!

Thirteen-year-old Rachel: Okay... Do you have friends at the job? Like, a group that you like to sit with during lunch?

Twenty-three-year-old Rachel: Well, most of them play poker while I sit alone in my office and eat mashed potatoes. Anyway, after lunch, I go back in the room, we talk for a few more hours, the day wraps up, the cool guys stay and play more poker, I go home, make dinner, and cry. And that's my day! Living the dream.

Thirteen-year-old Rachel: It sounds like you're being bullied.

Twenty-three-year-old Rachel: No no no no no. I'm not being bullied because sometimes the guys ask me to play poker with them and then point out when I'm doing it wrong. Also, I'm not being bullied because the guys who are assholes openly call themselves assholes. That's way too self-aware for them to be bullies! If their behavior makes me scared and intimidated and forget how to talk and weirdly become a worse writer the longer I'm at this job, well, that's on me.

Thirteen-year-old Rachel: Is there anyone at the job who doesn't make you scared?

Twenty-three-year-old Rachel: Totally. The bosses and some of the older writers are passively supportive before they also hole up in their respective offices during lunch. And, what's funny is some of them also have some trouble getting a word in. But that's the hierarchy of a writers' room: It's a true meritocracy in which the funniest joke always wins.

Thirteen-year-old Rachel: I thought you said the hierarchy of a writers' room was based on experience.

Twenty-three-year-old Rachel: Eh.

Thirteen-year-old Rachel: So is it fun being the only girl?

Twenty-three-year-old Rachel: Well, they hired me to bring a "woman's voice" to the table, but, to be honest, it's a teensy bit hard to do that when my voice literally doesn't carry over twelve other male voices. And wanting a woman to speak her mind is good on paper, but when there's a date rape joke pitched, I'M not gonna be the only one to point out that it's offensive. I'm the newbie! Did I mention how grateful I am to have this job?

Thirteen-year-old Rachel: You did. So if this is the way writers' rooms usually are, then isn't something wrong with the system?

Twenty-three-year-old Rachel: Ugh, that's such a GIRLIE thing to say. The reason I was hired for this is because I'm TOUGH. In the past ten years, I've made it my mission to grow a thick skin, to show that I can HANG WITH THE

LOUD BOYS. And I'm slowly getting better at making fun of them back!

Thirteen-year-old Rachel: Sorry, this really sounds like something I just wrote in my diary today: "I am getting better at the art of insults." But I'm realizing now that people who are actually good at insults don't generally write things like that.

Twenty-three-year-old Rachel: Said by someone who can't HANG WITH THE LOUD BOYS. Unlike you, I'm totally getting better at insults. Here's what I said in a recent email exchange with some of the guys from work after even one of the nice guys insulted me!

"Way to fucking turn on me. Congratulations for jumping on that very crowded bandwagon." Then, "Did I go too serious on that last bit?"

Twenty-three-year-old Rachel: Zing-a-roo!

Thirteen-year-old Rachel: Listen, I'm only thirteen so what do I know, but that email chain looked like you were genuinely offended, shared your feelings, got embarrassed, and then tried to take it all back.

Twenty-three-year-old Rachel: Yeah, on second thought, it wasn't the BEST zing-a-roo. The next day in the room, I asked the guys if I got too real on the email chain, and one of them said, "Yeah, and you also turned on one of the nicest people in this room, way to go." The room got quiet for a moment and I then wrote the following in my notebook:

Twenty-three-year-old Rachel: It says: "What is this running theme of me not fitting in? It's gotta be me, right?"; then a bunch of self-portraits of me as some monsters; then the next page says, "I Want To Dissolve." Also, I wrote "Kite Eyes" on the previous page for some reason.

Thirteen-year-old Rachel: Your handwriting looks like a serial killer.

Twenty-three-year-old Rachel: That's not a journalistic question, Bob Woodward.

Thirteen-year-old Rachel: More to the point, all of this looks like something I could have written in my diary like, yesterday. Do you have any thoughts about that?

Twenty-three-year-old Rachel: Funnily enough, every day I go to this job, I feel like I'm thirteen again, and I don't even need a time travel neuron chamber!

Thirteen-year-old Rachel: Oh no, you brought up the structural device of this interview again.

Twenty-three-year-old Rachel: Sure did! So, do you think you have everything you want? You know, for the piece?

Thirteen-year-old Rachel: I guess so. Thanks for your time and, um…take care of yourself, okay?

Twenty-three-year-old Rachel: You KNOW I will.

Thirteen-year-old Rachel: No, I don't.

Twenty-three-year-old Rachel: Oh right. *I* know *you* will.

Thirty-three-year-old Rachel: Okay, we should end it here, this is starting to get confusing.

Thirteen-year-old Rachel: Whoa!

Twenty-three-year-old Rachel: Who the fuck are you?!

Thirty-three-year-old Rachel: Oh, I'm *you* twenty years from now and *you* ten years from now. But don't mind me, I'm just eavesdropping to write this whole thing down for my book.

Thirteen-year-old Rachel: Whoa, you're writing a book?

Thirty-three-year-old Rachel: Yeah! I'll send it back to you through the time travel neuron chamber once I'm done.

Twenty-three-year-old Rachel: Okay, I feel like we're getting a bit cavalier with all this time travel.

Thirty-three-year-old Rachel: Nah, it's cool, what could go wrong?

(Thirteen-year-old Rachel sprouts a unicorn horn.)

Thirteen-year-old Rachel: OH GOD!!!!! WHAT HAVE WE DONE?!!! WHAT HAVE WE DONE???!!!

THE ONE-QUESTION PERSONALITY QUIZ

1. Quick! Over there! There's a lion behind a bush! She's been stalking you all day and now she's about to go in for the kill! What are you gonna do?

A. Run.
B. Kill the person nearest you and offer them up to the lion instead.
C. Try to kill the person nearest you but then back out at the last second because you feel bad and also you have no idea how to kill anything.
D. Sorry, I can't concentrate because I'm distracted by this hypothetical lion being a lady.
E. Tell the lion that you understand that it's in her nature to be a predator, but you have your own hopes and dreams and really don't want to die. Can't you both work something out?
F. There is no lion.

If you answered:

A: You have gone with the most logical response. It's a damn lion; RUN. This applies to non-lion-related stressful situations; our bodies cannot tell the difference between a lion in a bush and a jerky co-worker, so our stress hormones trigger a fight-or-flight response that causes us to, well, fight or fly. I'm not a scientist, but I do know how to Google "science fight or flight response explanation." According to Professor Internet, it is scientifically hard to stay creative in stressful situations because our amygdala sends an emergency signal to our hypothalamus. This really makes sense as to why it's hard for some (me) to be creative in emotionally difficult writers' rooms. With our lizard brains searching for possible lion escape routes, who can free-associate well enough to pitch cum jokes?

B: Bravo! You've learned to master your stress response and turn your fear of the lion outward! After all, it's not important to defeat the lion if the lion is focused on the weaker people around you, right? With this mentality, you've learned to thrive in scary situations. You're probably also an asshole!

I used to think Option B people were motivated by the urge to be mean for meanness's sake. It wasn't until recently that I fully understood that, like those who choose Option A, Option B people are also motivated by fear. Case in point: two recent-ish conversations that I had with jerks from my past.

Megan came to a live show I did in 2012. She had been the most popular girl in seventh grade and was actually one of the people who paid Devon McElroy to ask me out. At the stage door, she explained that she'd been sober for four years and, in that journey, she'd been apologizing to people she felt she'd wronged throughout her life. She handed me some flowers and a card featuring a picture of flappers on the front with the quote, "Well behaved women rarely make history." I was so touched by the flowers and the on-brand card that I asked her if she wanted to grab coffee nearby.

When Megan and I got on the subject of middle school, you would have never known she was popular from the way she talked about her experience. Megan talked about it similarly to the way I do: She was miserable the whole time, she felt out of place in her own body, she was even struggling with OCD. (I almost questioned her if she meant actual OCD or if she was using the term in the casual way people often do, like, "Oh man, I'm so OCD I can't stand it when there are dirty dishes in the sink," but I decided this wasn't the time or place to bring up how people can inadvertently trivialize mental health issues.) From our conversation, I gathered that being popular was the one thing in Megan's life that gave her self-worth and that she was constantly afraid of that going away. Wow, I marveled, the Berenstain Bears were right: Bullies really do build themselves up by putting others down. I didn't say the

Berenstain Bears thing out loud because I didn't want Megan to make fun of me.

About a year ago, I had a similar conversation with Matthew, one of the mean dudes at my first comedy writing job. Matthew had sought me out because he'd heard me on a podcast talking about my experience at that gig and he wanted to make sure he wasn't one of the mean guys I was talking about. Not missing a beat, I said yep, he sure was! I then launched into a huge rant about how bad he made me feel, the hurtful things he said, how scared I was of him every day. As I UNLOADED on him, it felt like I'd had an eight-year soda burp brewing and it was finally coming up. But the burp was justice and the soda was also justice.

Matthew was shocked that I felt bullied by him. He said that he was so insecure and in his *own* head at that job that his effect on others was the furthest thing from his mind. He didn't know that he'd thrown me to a lion—he was just relieved not to get eaten himself.

You may say: Well, what if the only way to succeed in a comedy writers' room *is* to be cutthroat like Matthew? Aren't comedians known for being mean and snarky? If you can't handle that, doesn't that make you, Rachel, a weak li'l snowflake puss?

Well, fuck off. But I would have actually agreed with you—that is, until I started writing on the show *Robot Chicken*.

As you may know, *Robot Chicken* is a long-running stop-motion animated sketch show on Adult Swim. In my job interview for it in 2012, one of the head writers warned me that it would be a "tough room" so before my first day of work, I steeled myself for another rocky experience. Once again, I was going to be not only the youngest person in the room but the only girl (in fact, only the second girl the show had hired at that point).

But the head writer was wrong. The room wasn't tough; it was just unsentimental. To be fair, it wasn't a typical writers' room setup; every writer worked on their own sketches for most of the day and, in the afternoon, all of the sketches were compiled into an anonymous packet to be judged in a meeting by the head writers. One by one, the bosses went over each idea and said, "I'm a yes" or "I'm a no." There was no added "I'm a no and whoever wrote this sketch should never work in comedy again." Just "I'm a yes" or "I'm a no."

The way I fundamentally see comedy jobs, though, was changed during the show's "scripting" phase. That was when we'd all be pitching ideas aloud like a typical writers' room. This is where the job could potentially become toxic and mean.

Which brings me to a writer named Zeb Wells. Zeb was an experienced writer on the show whose sketches were consistently hilarious. During the scripting phase, he was unsurprisingly balls-out funny, as funny as any of the guys from my first comedy job, and like those guys he was loud, confident, and performative. However, he managed to do all that and NOT belittle those around him. He didn't interrupt people or monopolize the conversation and even built on other people's ideas. Some of this came from the fact he was already an established writer at the show and had nothing to prove, but also, Zeb just wasn't the type of guy to see being good at comedy as synonymous with taking a diarrhea dump on other people's heads.* Zeb proved to me that you didn't have to be mean to be a great joke writer.

C: Awesome! You've chosen "The Bloom Special." It's my favorite dish on the menu. Would you like a side of fruit or sweet potato fries with that cop-out?

I am perpetually torn between my inner rage and inability to articulate that rage. I've always been, I guess the word is "spunky," enough to know that I should stand up for myself. You know, get it girl, Aries is a fire sign, werk bitch, all that. But I've always been bad at translating the urge to fight back into a coherent takedown of my enemies. Aka, I'm terrible at rap battles.

One example of this inability to insult under pressure is the email I sent to some of the guys at my old job. I didn't have a good retort to one of the insults being lobbed at me in the email chain because I couldn't bury my emotions well enough to be clever in the moment. My anger was unpolished

---

* As I continued to work with the *Robot Chicken* crew on other projects, I met many other hilarious guys in that circle who also weren't dicks. Bonus: They also started to hire more women!

and unrefined and it's always been that way. I have memories from as early as second grade of trying to insult a bully back, failing miserably, and then physically lashing out at myself so that I wouldn't hit them and get in trouble. Like, actually hitting myself. In front of the bullies. It was...weird.

I'm pleased to say that I'm getting better at containing my rage and, when appropriate, turning that rage into coherent words. But, to be fair, this is because I don't feel as threatened by the world anymore. When I had that conversation with Matthew, I was no longer a twenty-three-year-old ingenue desperate to impress a higher-up; I was a woman in her early thirties with an established career and, fuck it I'll say it, was higher status than him now. When Matthew told me that my experience of him being a bully made no sense because he had nothing against me, I wasn't afraid to call bullshit on this; I had recently found out that he and some of the other guys from my first job had been on another job together and had watched the pilot of *Crazy Ex-Girlfriend* at work just to mock it. When he stammered an excuse, I interrupted with, "Look man, I don't really give a shit if you don't think I'm funny." And I meant it. I really meant it. Mmmmmm tasty.

D: Yeah, it's a lady lion. Female lions do the bulk of the hunting. What's your problem, man?

E: This is how I deal with most threatening situations and it works like, 70 percent of the time. Being honest disarms people. We are poorly trained on how to be open and vulnerable with even our closest friends, let alone our enemies. So when you lay yourself bare to another person, it shows them your mutual humanity and can soften them. This tactic has freed me to stop seeing my own vulnerability as weakness.

I sometimes fantasize about if this tactic would have worked in places like middle school or my first writing job. I wonder what would have happened if I'd asked the guys at that job out to lunch and told them they were mean and it made me feel terrible because I just wanted to learn from them. Or would it have worked if I'd turned to my middle school bullies and said, "Hey. I'm miserable, you're miserable. Middle school sucks for all of us. Let's not fight"? Maybe that tactic would have solved everything.

Or maybe it would have been like the 30 percent of the time this tactic *doesn't* work. Because sometimes, you just can't reason with a fucking lion. That's right, in this case, the bullies are also the lion. There are multiple lions. In this story, not in the wild because they're endangered. Which is actually pretty sad because the world needs lions.

F: This is the only correct answer to this quiz. Oops, sorry to waste your time!

Unless you are staring down an actual lion, the "lion" is probably just a human being who's an asshole; a two-legged, weak, human being wearing a sweaty lion costume. If only we could all find the zipper at the back of that costume and expose their nakedness underneath. Figuratively. Don't try to disrobe your bullies.

When I spoke with Megan and Matthew, their lion costumes had long since disappeared for me. I was clearheaded and completely in my body during those two interactions. I said goodbye to Megan with my full forgiveness and a hug. (Well, first she asked me to be her acting mentor and I said I'd have to think about it, but, after that, there was forgiveness, then a hug.) I left Matthew by telling him to look out for the little guy.

I don't expect that I'm always going to be able to see through every lion. And I'm never gonna be good at "zing-a-roos." It's just not who I am. Sometimes, Option A (to run) is still the best option because why waste your time fucking with a lion?[*]

---

[*] Another caveat to the fellow members of the bullied squad: I should say that this quiz is based on my own experiences with the bullies/lions in my life. I am SO FUCKING LUCKY that these bullies/lions haven't threatened me physically, sexually assaulted me, or been in a position of power and made me fear for my job. If this is something you're going through and are earnestly looking to this book for guidance, this is an example of the 30 percent of the time when reasoning with a lion WILL NOT WORK. In cases like that, illegally poach the lion and nail their pelt to the fucking wall. Again, I mean a human lion, not a lion lion. Save the lions.

PART 8:

NORMAL PEOPLE MAKE NORMAL TELEVISION SHOWS

ALINE, HOLD MY UNDERWEAR

I cannot emphasize enough how unprepared I was for *Crazy Ex-Girlfriend* to be ordered to series. On May 3, 2015, it was a dead Showtime pilot and on May 10, 2015, I was boarding a plane to New York City to announce the TV series to press. In a town with the motto "Hurry up and wait," this time line was *blindingly* fast.

Nothing was normal[*] about the process of making *Crazy Ex-Girlfriend*, but its origin story is exceptionally weird and rare. In order to give you some context of how weird it was, here's how a new network TV show usually comes to be (the following typically takes place over the course of eight months):

- Pitch show to networks.
- If a network is interested, they pay you to write a pilot script.

---

[*] Staying on brand fuck yeah fuck yeah.

- If they like the pilot script, they shoot the pilot.
- While waiting to hear if the network likes the pilot, interview writers, directors, and department heads in preparation to go to series.
- Get ordered to series, feel pretty prepared.

And now here's how *Crazy Ex-Girlfriend* happened (the following takes place over *twenty* months):

- Pitch show to networks.
- Showtime orders the pilot script.
- Showtime loves the pilot script and says they will shoot the pilot if a big-enough director is found.
- Big-enough director found.
- Shoot pilot with the full support and enthusiasm of the network behind us and are told we are most likely going to get ordered to series.
- Thinking she's about to be a big fancy Showtime star, Rachel purchases a $10,000 wedding dress.
- Uh-oh, the notes came in and Showtime clearly doesn't like the pilot.
- We're taking their editing notes but oof it's not looking good.
- Showtime passes on the show the week of Rachel's wedding.
- Ouch bad timing.
- Rachel regrets buying expensive wedding dress.

- It's fine it's fine it's fine we'll just send the pilot to every other cable network it's so good someone will definitely want it.
- Every other cable network passes.
- Look into selling wedding dress.
- Rachel and Aline come to terms with the show being dead.
- Two months go by.
- Aline sees *Jane the Virgin* and thinks that maybe the CW might be a good fit, I mean, let's just send it to them what do we have to lose.
- Meet with the CW, they ask us to turn a version of the *Crazy Ex* pilot script into an hour-long show but no rush to turn that in because they're busy setting their shows for fall and won't be able to read our script until the summer.
- Do the changes for the CW right away so that we never have to think about this fucking show ever again and can move on with our lives.
- Turn in hour-long version of the pilot.
- Fuck show business.

And then, the following happens over the course of four days:

- Aline calls Rachel to tell her that, don't freak out, but the CW didn't like any of their fall pilots and *Crazy Ex-Girlfriend* is being considered for the fall schedule.
- One day passes.
- The CW has some last-minute notes that they want done ASAP so let's do them.

- Six hours pass.
- RACHEL THIS IS ALINE CALLING WE'VE BEEN ORDERED TO SERIES FOR FALL.
- What.
- What.
- Holy shit what.
- Oh my God we need writers.
- Oh my God we need directors and every other network TV show already has their directors set.
- Oh shit we haven't even told the cast yet, but Rachel, get on this plane to New York for this thing called UpFronts it's a long story no time to explain.

And with that, we were off to the races. As Aline was playing frantic catch-up on the showrunning side (putting together a writing staff, finding directors, hiring department heads), I was playing frantic catch-up on the TV-star side (smiling no matter what, being coherent at five in the morning, staying in a good mood even when a reporter asks me if I've ever "really been a *Crazy Ex-Girlfriend*" for the thousandth time). And with this new role, there were certain perks.

I started reaping the perks of my new reality the moment I boarded the plane. I had flown to New York from LA hundreds of times, but never in *first class*. Up until this point, my only interaction with first class had been to resentfully walk through it on my way to coach. I hated the rich fucks I saw, sipping their orange juices and stroking their emotional support Pomeranians. I took comfort in knowing that, if the plane were to crash, the people in first class would die instantly and cushion the blow for us in the back.

Now I was in first class, sitting in my luxuriously large seat with my feet not even touching the ground like a little girl's doll at a tea party. And I was PISSED. *This* is what flying has the potential to be? While most of us are sweating in the back and paying fourteen dollars for a stale croissant and a single Babybel, these first-class fuckers have *free socks* and *menus* and *reclining seats* and did I already say *free socks*?

And then someone brought me an orange juice and dammit, I couldn't be angry anymore. I drank Champagne. I slept. I reclined as I ate warm pie and watched *The Big Short*. Flying was awesome now.

Later, housing my free "Thanks for flying in first class" Milk Bar cookie, I walked through JFK pondering my next move. I could grab a cab into the city, but I was pretty broke, as evidenced by the fact I was staying with my friend Brendan[*] until the CW's free hotel room kicked in a day later. Brendan's place was on the Upper West, so I did the NYC subway math that I could take the A train into Manhattan and then transfer to the 2 at Columbus Circle and—wait, why does some dude in a suit have a sign with my name on it?

I forgot that I had a "car" "picking" "me up" at the "airport" (no words made sense anymore). I guiltily let the driver carry

---

[*] The duke!

my suitcase for me as we made our way to a big black SUV with a copy of *Town and Country* in the seat pocket. Later, I settled onto the air mattress in Brendan's apartment and relayed the day's events to my old trusted friend and he warmly replied as I expected he would: "Ugh, fuck off, you lucky bitch."

This lucky bitch fuckoffness continued with my first excursion to something called a "gifting suite." Every actor in town for UpFronts had been invited to this particular gifting suite and I was so excited. Maybe I'd get a free water bottle in a tote bag like those millionaires who give money to NPR! But when I walked into the suite, the free stuff was more than just a tote bag. In fact, it was a *lot* of tote bags. And if you can believe it, it *wasn't just tote bags.* There were racks of clothes open for the picking, a shoe store's worth of heels, purses galore, and makeup and hair products as far as the eye could see. As I loaded up my bags, I felt like Little Orphan Annie singing, "I Think I'm Gonna Like It Here." But in this version, it was about my ashamed delight at benefiting off the inherent unfairness of capitalism.

When I stepped onto the New York City Center stage for UpFronts rehearsal, my heart pounded as I read aloud from the teleprompter. A quick explanation of UpFronts: They are a yearly presentation in New York in which all the major networks present their new and returning shows for advertisers and press. It's the first glimpse anyone gets of new television shows and is apparently a big deal. Which is why it's shocking that I had been allowed to write my own speech for the

UpFronts presentation with no one bothering to even look at it beforehand. Somehow, the CW trusted me to just...say whatever I wanted and assume I wouldn't blurt out "tittyfuck" or something. This lack of oversight shows how much the powers that be were also scrambling to present this last-minute series pickup of *Crazy Ex-Girlfriend*.

This is also why no one had time to explain to me what the deal was with the red carpet before the presentation. I had no idea how to handle a red carpet, tips for the red carpet, how to pose on a red carpet, and that, hey, I would be on a red carpet so maybe I should get a stylist to help me with my clothes because that's what people did on red carpets.

When I found out at rehearsal that I actually needed *two* dresses for the day's events (one for the day stuff and another for the CW party at night), I didn't know what to do. I was only told to bring one dress for the whole shebang, so I brought my friend Nicole's mom's old Dolce & Gabbana dress from the eighties that she didn't want.

Then I remembered that I had all those free clothes I got at the gifting suite! Those clothes were definitely fancy enough—I hadn't had time to try them on, but they were from a gifting suite, and "suite" is a French word, so I was basically wearing French designer clothing! Perfect!

The morning of UpFronts, I got my hair and makeup done next to all of my fellow CW stars. Filled with adrenaline and punch drunk from a lack of sleep, I made chirpy conversation with everyone who caught my eye. Hi! I'm Rachel! What's your name? Wow, you're so attractive and you're so nice, you don't need to be this nice when you're this attractive! Hey, where ya goin'?

I went back to my room and threw on one of the dresses from the gifting suite along with a pair of heels that Aline had given to me because she didn't want them anymore (you may sense a fashion trend here). I looked in the mirror and thought to myself: Wow. I'm a TV star.

When I stepped out of The London hotel to my walk across the street to City Center, I was greeted by a mob of screaming fans...who couldn't have given less of a fuck about me. I scanned the crowd for literally anyone who wanted my autograph, but people peered past me for the CW stars on the shows they actually knew. I felt like a tree blocking a stop sign. As I walked away, I shouted back at the mob, "I have a show coming! I'm a CW star, too! You should care!"

Then I arrived at the entrance to the red carpet. Fun fact about red carpets: They're stupid. Nothing in life should be this frantic, loud, crowded, and fussy. As I stood there perplexed, I felt like an extra in some *Mad TV* sketch about Hollywood called "The Flash Flash Click Click Crew." The CW publicist and Gregor met up with me and the publicist asked if I was ready for pictures. I said I was and then my husband was politely asked to please walk behind the red carpet so he would not be seen by the press as he was not a famous person and therefore an eyesore.

Standing on the red carpet for pictures was overwhelming.

Cameras in my face, photographers screaming "Rachel! Rachel!" Wow. This *Mad TV* sketch was really one-note. And it occurred to me that I didn't know what the fuck I was doing. I didn't know how to pose, how to smile, how to step to the left so Grant Gustin could now get his picture taken. Plus, I had a coffee shit attack brewing and I still had half an hour of on-camera interviews to do. The inklings of imposter syndrome were brewing within me along with my coffee farts.

When I settled into my dressing room alone, I was grateful for a moment to breathe. But then another publicist I'd never met before (or maybe I'd met her five minutes ago, honestly I had no idea) walked in. Before I could ask her how long it would be until the presentation, she closed the door and asked, "Hey...do you have another dress?"

Um. What?

"You look BEAUTIFUL, it's just that we were wondering if you had something like, darker and more fitted because it will photograph better. Since we're so close to your hotel room I thought I'd ask."

I was stunned. And devastated. I thought I looked pretty. I thought I had fit in. But I guess I was wrong.

I then experienced the following revelatory thought process over the course of five seconds.

- Wait, did I just look like shit on my first red carpet?
- Oh no, am I gonna be in one of those "worst dressed" pictures in *Us Weekly*?

- Whatever who cares I don't care about looks because normalcy is bullshit or something like that.
- But I do care. I don't want to be ironically pretty right now. I want to be pretty pretty.
- Fuck, am I shallow? Am I like Tiffany and the Gaskins now?
- It's just like my fifth-grade teacher said. Normal kids don't dress the way I do.
- Oh no, I might cry.
- Huh. Tears aren't coming.
- Wait. In this potentially emotionally triggering situation am I...okay?
- I mean, the whole day has been potentially triggering for all of my insecurities. But I've mostly been okay!
- Yeah!
- Yeah!
- ...
- Yeah!
- And you know what? I can see myself in the mirror and I know for a fact that I look pretty good.
- I mean, maybe the dress is a little baggy.
- So if the dress is a little baggy and it's just a dress, is it that big a deal?
- Especially because fashion is a costume because everything is a costume because I stated before that social norms are ridiculous.
- So if it's a costume and I'm an actor here to play a role and right now my role is fancy TV star, fine I'll change.

"You know what? I actually do have another dress. I can change it's not a big deal."

The publicist sent a PA to my hotel room to grab another dress from the gifting suite as well as some Spanx. When the PA returned less than five minutes later with all of it, I immediately stripped naked. It was about this time that Aline walked into the dressing room to wish me luck. "No time to explain," I said, buck naked and squeezing into Spanx. "Hold my dirty underwear." I handed Aline my dirty underwear to hold as I put on the new outfit.[*]

Ten minutes later, I stood on the stage of New York City Center. As the head of the CW said, "Ladies and gentlemen, Rachel Bloom," a huge LED curtain rose to reveal... me. If the red carpet seemed like a *Mad TV*–style exaggeration of Holly-wood, this moment was out of some play I would have written in third grade about what I wanted to be when I grew up. And when I spoke to all twenty-eight hundred people using the speech I wrote, I didn't feel like an imposter, and it wasn't just because I put on a new dress. I felt like myself; even if I'd been wearing a trash bag, I still would have felt like I was exactly where I needed to be in that moment.

At the end of UpFronts, every cast member of every CW

---

[*] The Spanx were completely wrong because they were those skirt-style ones that ride up easily but that's what happens when you ask a super-skinny person to choose shapewear.

show went out onstage to wave goodbye to the crowd. I stood at the end of a long line of people, smiling and waving in all my short glory. And then…three tall men stepped in front of me. They were on a beloved CW show and were clearly more famous than I was and certainly more high status. It was understandable that they wouldn't notice I was there.

I was faced with a choice. Do I honor my position as the new kid on the block and let them step in front of me or—

Fuck it. I'm not even gonna pretend I was faced with a choice because of course I instantly stepped in front of *them* and kept on waving.

When I got back to my hotel room, I thought, *Wow, what a day*. It was a good learning experience but I'm so glad I'll be more prepared for next time. The thing is, though, so many things with *Crazy Ex-Girlfriend* over the next four years also had this kind of slapdash, seat-of-your-pants, make-it-up-as-we-go-along feel. Our season three premiere party was at an Olive Garden. Our sports bar set was converted into dozens of different music video settings because we'd always want to do the most expensive numbers right when we were out of money. It wouldn't even be the last time that Aline held my dirty underwear in her hand.

Four years later, the *New York Times* came to the *Crazy Ex* set to take a photo of me and Aline. It was accompanying a new piece they were doing about our partnership. As in the UpFronts four years previous, I was told to bring something nice to wear.

By that time, I had a stylist, and she picked out the perfect outfit for me to wear with perfect heels and perfect jewelry.

But I didn't want to fucking wear it. I had been shooting all day and my feet were tired and I could feel a pimple sprouting because my hormones were so fucked from the wonky travel schedule and I was behind on writing a song which I couldn't do because of this stupid photo shoot. I didn't want to fake a smile and pretend to be something I wasn't. I didn't want to hide my exhaustion because the exhaustion was the work and the work was the point.

So I said to Aline and all the publicists, "I'm gonna wear this sweatshirt for the *New York Times* photo shoot. I will wear no shapewear under it."

And they all said, "Good with us."

HELLO BATHROOM MY OLD FRIEND

There is so much to say about the experience of making the show *Crazy Ex-Girlfriend* that if I wanted to tell even a quarter of the stories from that time, it would take up a whole other book. But since writing another book right now sounds like getting a pap smear in a World War I trench, I'm gonna focus on one aspect of that experience for now. And that is: The Bathroom.

During *Crazy Ex-Girlfriend*, my ability to decompress in the bathroom was essential to my mental health. You might say that it made me feel…normal.* In many ways, I haven't changed since the days I wandered around in my diaper, pontificating and dreaming. The bathroom remains a sacred and creative space for me and during my days at *Crazy Ex*, it was the only place I could be alone. And as the show's star,

---

* Fuck yeah staying on brand some more fuck yeah.

co-creator, co-songwriter, music video script writer, and chief donut eater, I was NEVER alone.

But in the bathroom, I didn't have someone futzing with my hair or touching up my dark circles or sticking a freezing hand down my shirt to adjust my mic pack. I didn't have to read a script or watch an episode cut or make conversation with someone's agent who was visiting the set. ("Wow, that *does* sound like a fun acquisition!") In the bathroom, I could forget for a moment that 250 jobs depended on my ability to do mine. I could pretend for just a moment that no one needed me for anything...until I got a text message saying "Where u at we r waiting 4 u on set" at which point I would of course hurry to set and apologize for the delay.[*]

To show you how instrumental the bathroom was to my self-care while working on *Crazy Ex-Girlfriend*, below is a sample schedule of a typical workday.

5:30 a.m.: Wake up. Oh no. It's still dark outside.
6:30 a.m.: Call time. Goals to accomplish during hair and makeup: Eat breakfast, read an episode outline that Aline sent me, watch the latest cut of a music video, rehearse lines. Realistically what happens: Eat breakfast and fall asleep. Only wake up when my eyelashes are being curled. Fall back asleep after.

---

[*] I actually spent so much time in the bathroom that I later found out my pee breaks were always taken into account by the assistant directors when scheduling the scenes each day.

7:50 a.m.: BATHROOM BREAK #1. Not only is this morning pee essential, it's how I get my bearings after that long sitting-up sleep I just had. Without this bathroom break, I would be taking people by the shoulders and screaming Ebenezer Scrooge–style, "Tell me, good sir: what day is it?!"

8:00 a.m.: Go to set, rehearse the first scene.

8:15 a.m.: Get into costume, answer emails, rehearse my lines, basically do all the shit I was supposed to do in hair and makeup before I fell asleep. Berate self for falling asleep until I'm interrupted by a . . .

8:20 a.m.: BATHROOM BREAK #2. During my first shit of the day (breakfast-induced), I can take a deep breath and stop berating myself. (Poo-Pourri is essential for taking a deep breath at this moment.)

8:40 a.m.: Begin shooting first scene. Anytime the camera is not actively rolling, however, I have to either go into the writers' room OR go to editing to work on the latest music video OR write a song OR script a music video OR go to a costume fitting. I am so used to costume fittings by now that I don't even clock when I'm naked anymore. Sometimes, the costumers have to remind me to put my clothes back on before I walk out of the room.

9:40 a.m.: BATHROOM BREAK #3. Jesus Christ I need some space I'm tired of being naked I am so cold and the bathroom is the only irrefutable excuse for me to get

people off my ass for five fucking seconds. Take a breath, remind myself how lucky I am. Shed a single tear. Check Instagram. Get a text that says "Hi we saw you were posting on Instagram does that mean ur ready to come back to set?"

9:50 a.m.: Continue to shoot the first scene.

10:01 a.m.: BATHROOM BREAK #4. Sudden and urgent shit attack (coffee-induced).

10:10 a.m.: Feeling absolutely buoyant from the bucket of tar my body just released, I happily skip back to set only to find out we are behind schedule because of my shit attack.

12:10 p.m.: BATHROOM BREAK #5. I tell myself it's just a routine pee. But we all know it's gonna be more than that. The AD sighs.

12:20 p.m.: Shoot more.

2:00 p.m.: Lunch. Try to write a song while eating. No ideas are coming to me. I am a failure. I can't write anymore. I'm out of ideas. It's finally happened.

2:30 p.m.: BATHROOM BREAK #6. Go into the bathroom before I break it to everyone that I no longer have the ability to write. Pee, instantly feel better, and think of a great song idea. Pitch it to Adam and Jack and they like it, too, so I start to write the song on my phone until I get a text saying, "Where u at we r waiting 4 u in hair and makeup."

2:40 p.m.: Nap in hair and makeup because who are we kidding? I'm not getting any work done in there.

3:00 p.m.: Go to shoot a music video.

4:00 p.m.: BATHROOM BREAK #7. I kinda have to pee but it's also an excuse to talk to Aline for the first time that day. She and I speak while I'm on the toilet like I'm some low-stakes Lyndon Johnson.

4:10 p.m.: Continue to shoot the music video. Forget all the choreography I learned the day before.

5:00 p.m.: BATHROOM/CRY BREAK.

5:30 p.m.: Need a makeup touch up from the mascara stains on my cheeks. Respecting my privacy, no one asks me any questions. After five seconds of silence I blurt out, "Sorry about the mascara running down my cheeks, I've been crying from stress." As a boss, I believe in absolute transparency.

5:40 p.m.: Music video actually goes fine. Don't know what I was so worried about. I'm such a silly billy! Hahahahahahahaha.

6:40 p.m.: BATHROOM BREAK #9 because I can't stop laughing.

7:00 p.m.: Wait, I still have to shoot more stuff?! Fuck.

8:00 p.m.: Wrap. Prepare to go home and then realize that I still have to write that song that I tried to write on my phone earlier.

8:01 p.m.–?: BATHROOM BREAK #10. Write all of the lyrics while still on the toilet.

?:00: Oh shit, call time for tomorrow is in three hours?! **BATHROOM/CRY BREAK.**

THANKS FOR YOUR HELP IN BEATING THE SYSTEM, CHILD ME!

The pilot of *Crazy Ex-Girlfriend* featured a topless stripper and a graphic handjob scene. So obviously, some things had to change when we transitioned to the CW, a broadcast network. Like CBS, NBC, et cetera, a broadcast network is free for anyone to watch, including children, which means that any show airing on it must adhere to the censorship guidelines set by the FCC.

It was an adjustment going from edgy cable to broadcast—and to make things more confusing, the only guideline the FCC officially has is that "federal law prohibits obscene, indecent and profane content." This means that, outside of the obvious no-nos (saying fuck, shit, tits, showing fucking, shitting, or titting), the idea of "obscene, indecent and profane" content is open to legal interpretation. The bottom line is that if the FCC receives a complaint about a show and they rule that it's valid, a network can then be fined up to half a million dollars.*

I've spoken a lot about how connected I still feel to the child that I once was. Perhaps this is because, being an only child, I often did things with my parents that they wanted to do. For instance, my family and I watched a LOT of broadcast TV. Every week, my mom would record our favorite shows** on the same VHS tape and then we'd watch all of them on Friday night. (Yes, this means my family invented binge watching, and no, Netflix hasn't thanked me yet by buying any of my TV show pitches. In protest, I've held on to the same DVD of *Mr. Saturday Night* that I rented from them five years ago and I never intend to return it.)

In adapting the show for broadcast, I recalled all the times a character on one of my beloved shows said a line, and my parents laughed guiltily and I went, "What? What's so funny? What? WHAT'S SO FUNNY TREAT ME LIKE AN EQUAL!" Once I realized that the trick to getting around the rules of the FCC was to write jokes that would make sense to adults but fly over the heads of children, I became the standards and practices whisperer. Whenever a joke was flagged by S&P, I would ask myself if I would understand

---

*   If you're around my age and wondering how *NYPD Blue* got away with showing an ass and *Chicago Hope* got away with saying "shit," I've heard that the networks factored the FCC fine into the show's budgets.

**   Depending on the year, we're talking *The Nanny, Frasier, Seinfeld, Friends, Mad About You,* and *Everybody Loves Raymond.*

the joke if I was nine years old. As a result, it became my job to call the lovely head of S&P, Patricia, and plead our case.

Some examples of jokes child me helped us get away with:

1. The episode: 206

The joke: When in bed with Trent and deciding to have sex with him again, Rebecca pushes his head beneath the covers and says, "Nope, first you pay the toll, buddy." He then responds, "This is my favorite!"

S&P's argument: Hell no are you putting this on broadcast television.

My argument about what a kid would think: All a kid would think is that Rebecca was pushing Trent down toward her feet! Nine-year-old me would have interpreted it to mean that Rebecca wanted him to kiss her toes. Plus, "pay the toll" infers a literal form of payment. So maybe he was putting a dollar in between her toes. And maybe if we talked about female pleasure as much as we did male pleasure this wouldn't be a legal risk but thanks to the fact we come from British religious fanatics any sex act solely relating to female pleasure is still under the radar. So come on, S&P!

Outcome: SUCCESSFUL.

2. The Episode: 204

The joke: "Let's finish on her chest!" (from the song "We Tapped That Ass")

S&P's argument: Hell no are you putting this on broadcast television.

My argument about what a kid would think: A kid would just think they're finishing the song by dancing on a chest of drawers! It's perfectly innocent! YOU'RE the creeper reading into this, S&P!

S&P's counter-argument: Hmm. Can Rebecca be the one who delivers the joke so that it can say, "Please not on my chest, you'll scratch it?"

Me: Uh, okay.

Outcome: SUCCESSFUL.

3. The episode: 302

The joke: "*I say 'You're so mean!' / But dude, I'm so wet.*" (lyric in "Strip Away My Conscience")

S&P's argument: Hell no are you putting this on network television.

My argument about what a kid would think: As you can see in the script, Rebecca will dump a bucket of water on her head so that she's literally wet!

S&P's counter-argument: Rebecca dumping a bucket of water on her head is not organic to the song. We're onto you.

Me: Fuck. Okay, I have another joke to pitch you.

Outcome: Joke successfully CHANGED to "*Let me be your pupil / Let me choke on your cocksuredness.*" Children across America successfully protected from smut.

4. The episode: Also 302

The joke: *"Can't believe she didn't come... to tell me that she needed so much more than I could give."* (lyric from "The Buzzing from the Bathroom")

S&P's argument: Need to hear the song first.

My argument about what a kid would think: Here's the song! *(plays the song for S&P)* As you can see, the "come" joke is in one continuous sentence!

Outcome: ACCEPTED. Children across America successfully taught how to please their wives.

5. The episode: 206

The joke: *"Period Sex / Period Sex / If you're grossed out, just pretend it's cherry lube."**

S&P's argument: Hell no are you putting this on network television.

My argument about what a kid would think: Yeah I got no counter-argument on this one I just hoped you wouldn't notice.

Outcome: REJECTED.

6. The episode: 302

The joke: *"All female orgasms come from the clitoris."*

---

* To Patricia's credit, she DID allow repeated references to "periods" and "period sex" even when her co-workers balked. Her argument to THEM was that periods were a natural part of a woman's reproductive cycle and to talk about them was in no way gratuitously obscene. BLEED ON, PATRICIA, BLEED ON!

S&P's argument: Although we want you to be able to say this, we have been advised by outside legal counsel that the word "clitoris" cannot be said on this network.

My argument about what a kid would think: IT DOESN'T MATTER WHAT A KID WOULD THINK. THE CLITORIS IS A PART OF A WOMAN'S BODY AND IT IS NOT GRAPHIC OR INDECENT TO STATE ITS PURPOSE.

S&P's argument: You're right. Hmm. What if we made the scene, like, super scientific? So that it's plainly stating the facts and only the facts?

Us: So if someone literally holds up a scientific article that says 70 to 80 percent of women can only achieve orgasm from the direct stimulation of the clitoris, we can do it? Sure.

Outcome: ACCEPTED. My in-depth reading of *What's Happening to Me?* has finally come full circle.

PART 9:

NORMAL PEOPLE ARE CHILL WITH FAME

THE NIGHT THAT I WON A GOLDEN GLOBE AS DESCRIBED BY MY DOG WHO COULDN'T GIVE LESS OF A SHIT

Ahem. Testing, 1, 2. Is this dog-to-English translator working? Good.

I'm here to talk about *that night*.

Ever since *that night*, the Lady has been prancing around like she's better than me. But now I'm here to set the record straight. For she is not better than me. Wiley is queen. Wiley is supreme. To be clear: I'm Wiley.

You'll notice, first of all, that I don't call the Lady "Mommy." That's because she not my mommy. The Man is. In my head, the man is Mommy Man and the lady is Stepdad Lady. That because when they both rescued me, they were in something called a "long-distance relationship." I know, that phrase gross to me, too. Anyway, although I met the Lady on that day they rescued me, Lady went back to the other city she lived in and it was just me and Mommy Man.

To be clear: Yes, I'm a rescue, but I'm not a victim. Who rescued who? The answer is: Wiley rescued Wiley.

I like Stepdad Lady fine, but I love Mommy Man so much more. My favorite thing is to lick Mommy Man's feet. I can lick Mommy Man's feet for hours. Stepdad Lady's feet not as stinky so I only lick them for a sort of aperitif before Mommy Man's feet. I do, however, love the crotch of Stepdad Lady's dirty panties, but she no leave them on the floor for me anymore. Bummer for Wiley. Wiley love feasting on a woman's healthy and natural discharge.

I've heard rumors that Stepdad Lady has an impressive "career," but me not know what that means. I don't even know what Mommy Man's name is, let alone Stepdad Lady's name. I don't know where Mommy Man and Stepdad Lady go all day and I don't know where they hunt for all of my food. When Wiley have it good, Wiley no ask questions.

All I know is that, for a while, Mommy Man left during the day and Stepdad Lady had nothing to do but sit around the house, mutter to herself, leave messages for her agents that didn't get returned, and give me lots of walks. And then one day, Stepdad Lady is gone a lot more. She come home smelling sweaty and tired with strange paint on her face talking about "being on set all day." Me try to lick the face paint off. She let me for ten seconds, then say, "Ugh, your muzzle smells like old Thai food." Okay then, fuck off. Then Stepdad Lady washes herself in the dreaded WATER CAVE and comes out with less interesting clean smell and then doesn't even have the courtesy to leave her dirty panties on the ground.

RUFF! RUFF! RUFF! THERE'S A FUCKING SQUIRREL OUTSIDE! A FUCKING USELESS SQUIRREL! I WILL RIP OUT YOUR SPLEEN AND FORCE-FEED IT TO YOUR CHILDREN YOU AMPLE-BALLED FUCKING MOTHERFUCKER GET THE FUCK AWAY FROM MY HOUSE AND MY FAMILY!

Sorry. Where was I? Oh right. *That night.*

That night, Mommy Man and Stepdad Lady had been away for a long time. I know this because their scent disappeared in the house in the way that it does only when they gone for hours. So then, they come in da house smelling of excitement and Champagne and Stepdad Lady is holding some sort of hard golden toy in her hand. She kneels down and says, "Mommy just won a Golden Globe, Wiley!" Uh 1. I don't know what that is. 2. You not Mommy. 3. Gold toy too hard for Wiley to chew and destroy. 4. Gold toy is trash.

Then we go to sleep, but Stepdad Lady insist on putting Gold Toy next to me to make it look like I love Gold Toy. She take out square electric box, put in my face, then say something about "Gotta put this pic on Instagram." She say that a lot. Whatever. She finally take the stupid toy away. I lick my pussy, I lick my asshole, I lick Mommy Man's feet, I lick Stepdad Lady's face just so she won't feel left out, then I go to sleep.

And that's the story of the night Stepdad Lady got the Useless Gold Toy. She so weird sometimes.

Me with Trash

MY REVIEW OF AWARD SHOWS

When I took my parents to the Critics' Choice Awards in January 2019, they were STARSTRUCK. Look at the cameras! The gowns! Lady Gaga!

At first.

The magic started to wear off as we struggled through rush-hour-level foot traffic on the red carpet, couldn't find our table until after the awards started, and had to walk fifteen minutes to find any bathroom. After I inevitably got Maiseled and lost in my category to Rachel Brosnahan, we decided to leave. We felt a little shitty doing so . . . until we ran into all of the other fellow losers in the parking lot who were also peacing out. One of them even said, "I'm so cold and I just wanna go home to my cats."

So since people always ask me what it's *really* like to be at these award shows, below is a reviews system based on the things that TRULY count: Food, Parking, Temperature in the Room, and How Much Shapewear Is Expected.

THE EMMY AWARDS

Venue: The Microsoft Theater

Years attended: 2015, 2016, 2017, 2019

No, years you attended the REAL Emmys, not the Creative Arts Emmys: I mean they're the same experience but if you want to be that way just 2017.

Food: Drinks and mediocre snacks available for purchase at ridiculously elevated prices. Bring peanuts and a flask and save yourself $50.

Parking: Not great. The lots are really far away from the venue. Uber recommended; Razor scooter ideal.

Temperature in the room: Freezing. Bring a jacket. Not a "shawl." I mean a full-on Patagonia.

How much shapewear is expected: A medium amount. These awards are in September, which means it's right at the end of swimsuit season so you may be able to coast on your summer bod if you had one. If not, you're *totally* gonna get it together before next summer and this time you mean it!

THE GOLDEN GLOBES

Venue: The Beverly Hilton

Years attended: 2016, 2017

Food: Full meal AND free alcohol at this awards show! Not even that cheeky scoundrel Ricky Gervais can trash that!

Parking: Nonexistent. To even attend one of the after-parties, you have to park in a lot miles away and take a crowded bus to the venue. And even when you have clearance to drive right up to the red carpet, you're still stuck in traffic for thirty minutes as police inspect every car (but obviously turn a blind eye to the excellent cocaine being brought in by half the attendees).

Temperature in the room: A brisk autumn day. Bring a light sweater.

How much shapewear is expected: A huge amount. These awards are a formal event right after the holidays and the Patriarchy demands that after a binge we must immediately purge.

THE TONY AWARDS

Venue: Radio City Music Hall

Years attended: 2017, 2018

Food: NOTHING, but that's the theater for you.

Parking: N/A because "I'm walkin' here!"

Temperature in the room: Mildly chilly; freezing in 2017 when host Kevin Spacey launched into his Johnny Carson impression.

How much shapewear is expected: It's the end of awards season so everyone is a little more forgiving. However, if you don't want to look like a house standing next to a Rockette, I suggest either a whalebone corset or a caftan.

THE CRITICS' CHOICE AWARDS

Venue: The Barker Hangar

Years attended: 2016, 2017, 2019

Food: Not great and also not enough of it. Pack a purse big enough to hold multiple sandwiches. Either a Birkin or a plastic bag will do.

Parking: It's drive-up only but I bet you can ask to put your Razor scooter by the entrance.

Temperature in the room: FREEZING. The awards show is in winter by the beach in a former airplane hangar. This means that the whole thing is a "Let It Go"–esque frozen abyss. Plus side: You can fully do the thing where Elsa watches her glove fly into the air.

How much shapewear is expected: A moderate amount. It's right after the holidays but it's less important than the Golden Globes, which happen very close to this awards show, so people are kind of shapewear-ed out. Ultimately, the less high status you feel in Hollywood at this moment, the more shapewear you'll want to wear at this show.

Case in point, my intense shapewear at the last one I went to:

PREP

RESULT

WORTH IT?

THE SHOW MUST.
GO. ON.

As I've stated over and over again, I am a theater kid. That means I'm desperate to be the best, desperate to please, desperate to never let anybody down. There is no room for failure, because failure equals weakness, which equals death. I've tried to adjust my mindset away from this, but old habits die hard. And when things get dire, man, sometimes only the energy of a show pony dressage-ing on a broken leg can get you through life.

Being a show pony is how I managed to pitch *Crazy Ex-Girlfriend* through that days-long anxiety spiral and how I managed the show's rigorous schedule. After *Crazy Ex* ended, though, I told myself that I would stop pushing through my emotions for the sake of putting on a show. From now on, I said to myself, I would put my health and happiness above everything.

But then, a couple of months later, it was the second night

of the Creative Arts Emmys. I was in a musical number that opened both nights of the award show because it was offered to someone way more famous but they turned it down. (I get a lot of gigs this way. Keep 'em comin'!)

The second night of the awards, I was on a high because my songwriting partners and I had just won an Emmy the night before. It was one of the greatest nights of my life. Jack Dolgen,[*] Adam Schlesinger,[**] and I had written 157 original songs for the series, and I had an unhealthy need for the validation of this award.

We were all hanging out in my dressing room and partying when the stage manager told me I had twenty minutes until the show started. I went into my bathroom to change into my show dress. As I took off my red-carpet-gown Spanx to transfer into my show Spanx (man, I couldn't wait to get home and put on my more comfortable pajama Spanx), I saw it.

Blood. Blood in the crotch.

Context: at the time, I was three months pregnant. The day before, off my Emmy-winning high, I announced the happy news to the world. So when I saw the blood in my Spanx crotch, my first thought was: Fuck. I jinxed it. I flew too close

---

[*] Jack and I have been writing together since "Fuck Me, Ray Bradbury," which he also produced. On CXG he was not only the co-songwriter but also an executive producer and director. A fun fact about Jack: He's co-written two books about menopause with his mother.

[**] Adam had won two Emmys already, but he wanted a third one to balance out the Emmy shelf. Fun fact about Adam: The song "Stacy's Mom" (which he wrote) was inspired by his own hot grandmother.

to the sun, and the evil eye that assumedly lives in the sun saw me flying by the sun and was like, "Oh no you don't, I'm a sentient eye, I'm coming to get you."

I stripped down entirely and sat on the toilet to do some literal digging. (Note: Gay men might want to skip this paragraph.) Maybe it was just dried blood that I saw in my Spanx? After all, I'd been spotting brown for the past few weeks (normal during the first trimester), so maybe this was just more of that. I put a wad of toilet paper against my vagina, held it there for a few seconds, then looked. The "putting toilet paper up to your vagina and hoping that there's blood" is a monthly ritual that some women reading this may know all too well. That little spot of red means we don't have to make a trip to Planned Parenthood this month.

For the first time ever, though, I didn't want to see the red spot in the toilet paper. But I did. And lots of it. This wasn't just a spot; this looked like a full-blown period.

I started to panic. I heard someone say "Fifteen minutes, Rachel!" like we were in a forties movie. I called my husband in to help me as if he'd know what to do. When that of course proved useless, I had him fetch the closest thing to an expert I could think of: my friend Sarah, who was hanging out in the dressing room with us and who had recently had an early miscarriage. Sarah came in the bathroom, completely unfazed to see me buck naked on the toilet with dried blood between my legs. She immediately knelt down to vagina level and I showed her the stained toilet paper as if she were my doctor.

Sarah looked at the toilet paper, took a big doctor-ey breath, and told me that, honestly, this wasn't a lot of blood. She'd learned a lot about miscarriages from her own recent experience and, in her opinion, this didn't look like one. Sarah calmly asked me if I'd had sex recently. Yeah, I answered, that morning, my husband really gave it to me good. Sarah asked me if I had any pain. I said no. She then said okay, the sex was most likely the cause of the moderate amount of blood she saw.

Slightly pacified by Dr. Sarah, I then had enough presence of mind to call the after-hours doctor at my gyno. No answer. I left a message.

I was faced with a choice. If there was, say, a 10 percent chance I was having a miscarriage, should I bail on the Emmys and just go to the emergency room? WAS there anything to do if I was having a miscarriage? How do miscarriages work?

When I heard "five minutes!" my show pony instinct kicked in. I numbly put on my costume, allowed myself to be mic-ed, and followed the stage manager up the stairs. I stood backstage and, from a distant land, heard someone say, "Please welcome last night's Emmy winner, Rachel Bloom!"

I walked onstage and did it. I did the number. I don't remember it at all, but it seemed to go fine. It went so fine that they used that night's performance on the official Creative Arts Emmys broadcast. I still haven't watched it. I don't want to see what I look like when I'm slapping a smile over terror.

When I got back downstairs after the performance, the bleeding had stopped. Dr. My-Friend-Sarah was right. I checked my phone and the on-call doctor had left a voicemail saying that, because I had no pain accompanying the bleeding, it was probably fine. If you're medically curious, I found out at the doctor the next day that the bleeding was caused by my amniotic sac momentarily separating from my uterine wall—something that is actually super normal in early pregnancy. Ms. Fetus was A-okay.

Did me going on with the show that night despite the bleeding exhibit good self-care? I don't know. If I'm really being honest with myself, going on with the show *is* sometimes how I care for myself. I love what I do. It makes me really happy.

Plus, if it *had* been a miscarriage, I don't think that abstaining from a two-minute musical number would have stopped it anyway, right? Right?

Right?

MY OFFICIAL CELEBRITY CAUSE

When one is fortunate enough to have a platform like I do, it's important to use that platform to spread awareness of meaningful issues. So I'd like to take a beat to talk about what's really important in the scheme of things: amusement parks.

Growing up in Southern California, the holy trifecta of Disneyland, Knott's Berry Farm, and Six Flags were staples of my childhood.* However, two things bother me about amusement parks now that I'm an adult:

---

* My family actually took the SoCal amusement park obsession one step further by getting a yearlong pass to Disneyland when I was in elementary school. This meant that, if my homework was done, we would make the forty-minute drive *on a school night*, haul ass into the park, fit in a few roller coasters, and then I'd fall asleep in the car. I spent as much time at Disneyland as anyplace in my actual neighborhood; my Main Street, USA, was literally Main Street, USA. One time, my parents and I even went on Yom Kippur. At one point, I remember my mother saying, "Who says we aren't at temple? We're at a temple...of the Forbidden Eye!"

1. Every ride is based on some sort of children's movie or TV show, and the older I get, the less I know of family-friendly pop culture. Like, I'm sorry, why would I ever voluntarily watch *Cars*?
2. Since amusement parks are geared toward children, the rides and attractions do not play to the top of my intelligence.

Here's my official celebrity cause: Amusement parks should be smarter. To rectify this problem I plan to start small with a yearly gala and a canned food drive, but my ultimate goal is to *create an original amusement park aimed at adults.* In order to do this, I will need a billion dollars. Obviously, the more famous I get, the more people will give me money to make this park. But until that day comes, I present to you the theoretical map for: Original Narrative Fun Times Thrill World.

Prepare your eyes for a
dazzling piece of art.

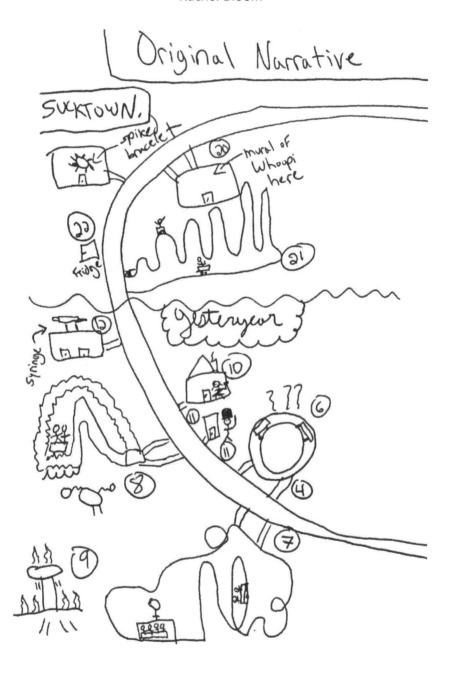

MAP KEY:

1. **Will Have a Focus Group for a Better Title Once I Get a Billion Dollars.**
2. **Character Sightings:** Every one of our costumed Cast Members is actually a medical doctor who you can ask about any random pains or weird moles. They will not pose for pictures.
3. **The "Haha, You Look Dumb" Photo Station:** Instead of classic ride photos, we have cameras throughout the park to take random pictures of you throughout the day. See what your face REALLY looks like when you scream at your husband!
4. **Our Patented Double Line System™:** Nope, that's not a FastPass line—it's a line just for adults! Sip calming cocktails in the adult line and watch the kids do whatever they want in their line via soundproof Plexiglas. (Legal waivers must be signed upon entry.)
5. **Edible Station:** No trip to our park is complete without a pit stop at our weed edible station. Get edibles timed specifically to kick in at the most thrilling moments of some of our favorite rides! *(Park not responsible for potential negative repercussions caused by the huge life revelations you may have during this intense experience.)*

YESTERYEAR
Rides and Attractions:

6. **The Lingering Odor Motors (Sponsored by Prius™):** Steer your own car-turned-time-machine into the past! From the Parisian Belle Epoque to a medieval joust to Victorian London, you can careen through some of your favorite historical scenes brought to life by set design, animatronics, and the realistic odors of what it would have smelled like back then! Hint: It's BO and shit!

7. **Girl Power!:** In this thrilling, upside-down steel roller coaster, you'll careen through the history of women's rights. But just as you've made real progress, something inevitably sets you back—backWARD, that is!

8. **The "Get Born" Rapids:** Grab a slicker and get ready to relive the day you were born! You'll start out by floating in a pink room with nothing but the sound of a heartbeat and the vague smell of Indian food because that's what your mom ate for lunch that day. Then get ready for a free-fall slide that takes you into a tight rubber tube that squeezes you from one to eight hours until you emerge in a lukewarm splashdown! (And waaaaaaatch out for the Abominable Snowman and his episiotomy scissors!)

9. **The Hindenburg Fiery Free Fall:** Oh, the Humanity—of Thrills! *(Note: A strobe light is used in this attraction.)*

Food:

10. **The Fifties Alabama Diner:** When you check in with the hostess, clarify your family background. Then watch how your race, religion, or sexual orientation affects the quality of your service. Ah, the good old days!

11. **Mama Gruna's Shtetl Dinner and Show:** Step back into a poor home in a Jewish shtetl in the 1800s for delicious home-cooked potatoes, onion soup, potatoes, ground fish, stale bread, and potatoes! Served buffet-style (in that each dish must be reluctantly taken from the hands of one of Mama Gruna's many children). And bewaaaaaare of the Cossacks hiding under each table! *(Vegan options available.)*

Shopping:

12. **They Didn't Know This Stuff Was Bad:** Shop like a person of history! Buy cocaine toothache drops, morphine teething syrup, and Dr. McKimball's Pep Pep Energy Fizzers (straight-up meth).

NOW-LAND
Rides and Attractions:

13. **The Anti-Haunted Mansion:** Get ready to shriek! This haunted house explores something even scarier than ghosts and ghouls—the prospect of *nothing* coming after death!

Grab your kids and travel from empty void to empty void symbolizing the endless, emotionless nothing of what is most likely everyone's fate. Can you say, "Boo"?

14. *Lost*: **The Ride!:** We couldn't resist basing ONE of our rides on an existing TV franchise. And what a beloved one it is! On the thrilling five-hour-long lift hill, relive some of the most thrilling moments in the television show with state-of-the-art animatronics and projections. Then prepare for a thrilling drop—that never comes! Like *Lost*, this ride was also leading to nothing the whole time. You'll want half your day back just like I want those six years back!

15. **How to Do Your Taxes:** What's the difference between a W-2 and a 1099? Don't worry, we got you covered! Kids of all ages will learn how taxes work, because no one else will show you! This is a thrilling stunt show with motorcycle and skateboarding tricks to keep you interested as a dry professor stands on a raised podium and explains tax law! I am in particular need of this attraction!

16. **Haruki Murakami's Bumper Cars:** Fasten your seat belts for a bumper car ride based around an original story by the novelist Haruki Murakami! It's a real fender/mind bender!

17. **Where It All Went Wrong:** Fill out a twenty-five-page questionnaire to embark on this personalized dark ride! Using lifelike animatronics, videos downloaded off your phone, and secret calls we'll make to your family and friends, you'll relive all of the worst decisions you ever made. Then, when the ride ends, you'll go through the ride AGAIN, but, this time,

you'll see what your life would be like if you had made better decisions! *(Edible station not recommended before this ride.)*

Shopping:

18. **Bring Your Own Clothes:** Most of the clothes sold at amusement parks are cheaply made and outdated (see: the hip-hop Tweety-themed gift shop at Six Flags Magic Mountain). But you still want a wearable memento of your special day, right? So bring any item of your own clothing into this store, give it to us, and we'll iron a park badge on it then sell it back to you for twice the price!

Food:

19. **Dole Whip:** Move over, Disney, we got it here, too! BECAUSE I HAVE A BILLION DOLLARS.

SUCKTOWN (For the Terrible People in the Group) Rides and Attractions:

20. **"Why Are You This Way?" The Movie:** Narrated by Academy Award™ winner Whoopi Goldberg, this movie explores why you're a terrible person whose friends had to dump you in this land. Why do you hate fun and, more important, insist on ruining other people's fun? Whether you hate amusement parks, hate sunlight, or just don't want

to be happy, you'll either leave this movie a better person or you'll just stay in the cool darkness of the theater all day rather than burdening the world with your presence.

21. **Intro to Roller Coasters: The Roller Coaster:** You've told everyone you hate roller coasters, but how do you know unless you try one? This fifteen-minute-long ride is a series of drops and loops that get bigger each time. Want to opt out? No problem! There are stations after every drop or loop that you can exit from. This is a legitimately good idea and if someone else copies this I will sue you WITH MY BILLION DOLLARS.

Food:

22. **A Kitchen with a Moderately Well-Stocked Fridge:** Make your own shit since you think you're so great.

Shopping:

23. **Hot Topic:** It's all you deserve.

KIDZ KORNER (For Ages 3 and Under) Attractions:

24. **A Bunch of Cardboard Boxes for the Kids to Tear Apart:** We'd rather not waste precious resources on an age group that can't form real memories.

THE QUEST TO MAKE EVERYONE LIKE ME: A FANTASY (OR: EAT, PRAY, CRY)

"YOU HAVE NO TALENT."

That's what the person on Twitter said. "YOU HAVE NO TALENT."

I read it again, making sure that the tweet didn't say "YOU HAVE NO TALENT AND ALSO IT'S OPPOSITE DAY!"

Nope. Just, "YOU HAVE NO TALENT."

This must be some mistake. I know for a fact that I, Rachel Bloom, do indeed have talent. Oh wait: This poor person must have me confused with someone else. Another Rachel Bloom who, unlike me, DOESN'T have talent. Poor thing. THAT Rachel Bloom should just give up and become a life coach or something sad like that.

But I checked again, and this tweet was the latest in a line of tweets from this person calling me and my TV show a self-indulgent mess.

Time stood still. My heartbeat sped up. I clutched the set of pearls that had suddenly appeared on my neck. Somewhere, a puppy burst into flame. If this "no talent" tweet was indeed written by a real person, it meant that the thing I had always dreaded was turning out to be true.

Not everyone in the world liked me.

I knew that this was true in the PAST. In the PAST, before I had my shit together, not everyone in the world liked me. I was a mess. But now, I'd fixed all of that and was perfect. I knew that you shouldn't pay attention to internet comments, but secretly, I assumed that advice was for *other* people. I'd even counseled those other people who were upset with internet comments by saying, "Hey man, art is subjective and everyone has their own experiences that color the way they perceive what you put out into the world. Just be yourself and fuck the haters!" But in the back of my head, I thought, "Except for me because everyone likes me and I'm adorable and amazing."

I'd been insulted online before, but those had always been comments left on YouTube music videos I'd done. Negative YouTube comments are easier to dismiss. Anyone who insulted me on YouTube, I assumed, was most likely a misogynist, anti-Semitic, super-religious professional anti-abortion speaker / monster truck rally hot dog vendor / baby elephant poacher who was going through a hard time with his failed penis enlargement surgery and also was a bot.

But this was different. This was a personal attack aimed at me and, not only that, it contained my and any artist's biggest fear: that I had no talent. And when any thought is converted into the written word, that makes it a true fact.

I ignored all the other lovely comments aimed at me on Twitter. No time for those meaningless words now. Stupid kind idiots. I had to know who wrote this insult, because they were obviously a genius.

I clicked on this person's profile. Nothing. No information. Their profile picture was just the default egg that usually meant either a fake account or a senior citizen. That night, I had a nightmare of being chased by a giant Twitter egg that was yelling my biggest insecurities at me. "You dance like you're still a virgin!" and "Everyone notices that you have a lopsided smile!" and "You're too much of a gluttonous fatass to ever become a vegan even though you know it's the ethical thing to do!"

I woke up the next morning, resolved to put this all behind me. One bad comment from a random person was just that: one bad comment. I was right when I had given others the advice to "ignore the haters"; the internet was notorious for trolls ruining everyone else's time. I even felt stupid for being hurt. But then, I saw another Twitter comment from another person. "Saw your show last night & u suck LOL"

What? I SUCK? HOW do I suck? Does the character I play suck? Did you do a bunch of research on me and come to the conclusion that I PERSONALLY suck? Or do we know each other? *Or* does the use of LOL negate the insult and imply that it indeed was opposite day?

I decided to do something about all this. Enough was

enough. I was gonna take a stand against internet bullying, specifically just my own internet bullying. I skipped work the next day to thoroughly scour the internet for anything bad that had ever been said about me. I had to film *Crazy Ex-Girlfriend*, of course, so to get out of it, I told everyone at work that I "had a seizure."

I formed a plan to change hearts and minds. First, I messaged every person who had ever insulted my talent or personality and asked for their Venmo or PayPal usernames. I then deposited $100 into each and every one of their accounts. When I found the person who wrote, "Saw your show last night & u suck LOL," I found out that she was a lady in Michigan who had started a GoFundMe for her grandma's hip replacement. I fully funded it. Within hours, I received a heartfelt email from her. "I am beyond words. From the bottom of my heart, thank you. I don't know if this is the same Rachel Bloom I tweeted at last night, but if it is... I had just gotten yelled at by my boss at Office Depot and when I saw your show, I got super jealous LOL."

So this was the proof. Everyone in the world DID like me, they were just taking their frustrations out on me! Thank GOD. I knew I was perfect. Emboldened by my great day on the internet, I not only messaged the original troll for his or her Venmo account information, but I also sent them a litany of my music comedy videos to prove that I, indeed, had talent.

I went back to work but had an assistant on retainer full-time just to monitor insults on my social media. Every time somebody posted a negative comment about me, or a negative tweet, my assistant would find out who it was, and I would then do something to win them over. If it was a person with a blog, for instance, I would openly post about the blog and say, "This is the greatest blog! Read this blog!" Over the course of six months, I bribed my way into the world's heart. I tweeted about new sandal brands, did Instagram stories congratulating random high school football teams on their win, and paid for prom dresses, surgeries, dog psychics, guns, you name it.

And in the course of doing this, I received words of gratitude from almost everyone. Everyone, that is, except for the person who said I had no talent. Fuck.

A month later, I still hadn't heard from this original "no talent" troll, so I of course skipped work again by telling my co-workers that the seizure had "turned into cancer." I had to ramp this search up a notch. People kept coming to my house to "check on me," so I set up shop at a local café where I could internet-stalk in peace.

There had to be something I was missing. Why did this person still not like me?

After an even deeper internet search, I found out that there was a lot of hate online directed at me for various political ideas I'd espoused over the years. Being pro-choice, pro-LGBTQ-rights, a believer in climate change, et cetera. Ugh, these thought-out principles were really boning me. So I messaged every conservative who had ever written a mean word about me, from Twitter users to writers of Breitbart columns, and told them that I was actually a secret conservative who was just spying on the liberals for information and would release a tell-all book someday about the liberals but please don't tell anyone because it would blow my cover but also stop writing mean things about me.

I also messaged this all to the person who said I had no talent, just to cover my bases. No word back, though.

Ignoring all the invites to Republican fundraising parties I was now receiving, I racked my brain. What else could I do to make *everyone* like me? Desperate times. I was faced with no other choice than to completely change who I was. I started scouring Reddit and every message board for every bad thing anyone had ever said about me. I took copious notes on what not to do and what not to be: "Don't be awkward," "Don't 'need to lose weight,'" "Don't be a Jew pedophile." These become my meditation mantras each morning.

At this point, production had fully stopped on *Crazy Ex-Girlfriend* while I "recovered" from my cancer-seizure-tapeworm illness (I added the tapeworm thing to really cover my bases). Production insurance needed a doctor's note to cover all of the money lost from halting production, but luckily one of the trolls who used to hate me was also a doctor, so he did me a solid and wrote a note. He was about to have his medical license taken away, so I got in there just in time!

I still hadn't heard from the person who originally said I had no talent so I hired a private detective. The detective said they couldn't find out who this person was without an official warrant to get their IP address, and they couldn't do that without an actual threat to my life. So I Photoshopped a fake screenshot of the person saying they were gonna bomb my house and sent it to the detective. I'm so smart.

Meanwhile, I decided that any public opinion of mine was too much of a risk, so I took anything potentially divisive I'd ever done or said off the internet, which was everything. Starting fresh, I recorded a new song called "Puppies Are Great." Can't argue with that, right? When *that* got a mean comment from a person who was clearly a bot, I recorded a follow-up called "Bots Are Cool."

A few months into my quest, there was a little snag. Remember how I told all those conservatives that I was a secret spy? Well, one of them wrote a think piece about it, of course, which then caused a bunch of liberals to write their own think pieces about how I was a "traitor to my views." But with the help of my private detective, I found out where each of the authors of each of the think pieces lived and I presented to them a giant blank check from a fund called "The Rachel Bloom Creative Grant for Those Who Write Think Pieces." These authors might have principles, but they were working freelance and I knew what those kinds of gigs paid. They were more than happy to take their articles down in exchange for money. Then, to lock them down for life, I started my own website called "Why I Love Rachel Bloom" and hired every freelancer to write for it. I'm *so* smart.

I was so close to making everyone in the world like me. But

then I realized: I couldn't make everyone in the world like me if not everyone in the world knew who I was. I was on a cult musical TV show that was a far cry from reaching everyone worldwide that I needed to. So I resolved to drop everything in my life and go to every town in every corner of the globe in order to rectify the situation.

Twenty years later, it seemed like I was pretty close to my goal. I'd been to every city, town, and hamlet on earth. I'd taught the elderly yoga, nursed sick babies back to health, even converted to every local religion to ingratiate myself. My husband had left me at this point, and I was replaced on *Crazy Ex-Girlfriend* by Lea Michele, but still, I felt pretty good.

The year is now 2050 and I can say with certainty that, short of those tribes in South America that will instantly kill any outsider, I am liked, nay, loved, by every single person in the world.

Except for one. That original person who said I had no talent.

Which brings me now to where I'm writing this: outside a shack in the middle of Finland. The private detective had said this was the address of the person who had written that comment all those years ago. They couldn't be prosecuted for the bomb threat because the police realized I had Photoshopped the whole thing. Oh, I was also wanted for fraud back in America.

I knock on the door. An old and gnarled woman opens it. Before I can say anything, she sneers: "I know why you're here.

I know why you've come so far. So let me say: I will never like you, Rachel Bloom. Never, ever, ever."

I get down on my knees and clutch her torn skirt. Why? Why? Was it something I said? Something I did? Something about my appearance? I can change it! I'll do anything, anything for her! Why doesn't she like me or think I have talent?

She replies, "Honestly, I don't know. It's probably a mix of you being annoying and my own shit. But regardless, I'm not a fan."

And that's when I realize: The world doesn't revolve around me. What if a stranger not liking me *isn't* the end of my life and existence and humanity? What if most people aren't thinking much about me either way because they're busy with their own lives? And if they are thinking about me, they carry their own biases and it's a waste of time to parse out which opinions about me are actual statements about me as a person and which just reflect their own experiences?

The lady starts laughing. And I start laughing. She and I are the same. We have always been the same. The concept of myself slipping away, the ground rumbles and I feel the universe around me start to implode.

Oh fuck. It turns out, I WAS the center of the universe, and letting go of my ego caused the universe to cease to exist. My bad.

As I watch the planets spin around me and I get sucked into the old woman's mouth, which has now become a wormhole, the last thing I hear is, "You have no talent. LOL."

NORMAL PEOPLE SAW THIS TWIST COMING

By the time I turned thirty, I should have understood that there was no such thing as "normal." But I still couldn't stop the little voice in the back of my head that occasionally whispered, "Freak." This is why I was terrified when I started to write more vulnerable songs for *Crazy Ex-Girlfriend*. I worried that the song "Stupid Bitch," based on some of my own worst moments, would be so self-loathing that no one would get the joke; that the song "A Diagnosis" would look too earnest and make me the laughingstock of the internet. Every time I penned a more earnest lyric, I needed the validation of Aline, Jack, or Adam to assure me that I wasn't humiliating myself.

And then we started doing live shows and I saw that the very songs I'd been the most scared to write were the songs that people connected with the most. As I watched thousands sing along and wave their phone flashlights to the lyric, "*You're just a poopy little slut who doesn't think and deceives the people she loves*," I thought, Holy fuck, I'm not alone. And when I met those fans afterward, they weren't just people who seemed like my friends; they seemed like...me. They didn't have to be girls with short torsos and triple D's wearing Deathly Hallows shirts for me to feel this kinship (although there were quite a few of those). No matter what they looked like, they all had one thing in common: They saw themselves as outsiders. And they were kind, smart, funny, generous, and fascinating.

So the big twist of this book...is you. By supporting me, you have inadvertently changed my life and made the title of this book irrelevant. Because maybe there *are* people out there who are "normal." But I don't need to be one of them. Not anymore.

A NORMAL AFTERWORD

I turned in my finished manuscript for this book on March 24, 2020, very pregnant and very satisfied with myself. It felt perfect that I finished a book all about my relationship with normalcy; after all, with a new human soon entering my life, my whole concept of "normal" was about to completely change.

But fuck, I had no idea.

As my due date drew closer, the COVID-19 pandemic was getting bad in the US, with New York City becoming the world's epicenter. Because of this, I was getting induced to get ahead of the potentially devastating Los Angeles hospital rush as well as a potential ban on fathers being in the delivery room. Despite the state of the world, I let my husband do the bulk of the "pandemic worrying" while I focused on basking in the glow of my finished book and debating which song from *Sunday in the Park with George* would work best on my birthing playlist. When we checked into the hospital, I had a mask on with a big smile beneath it.

But then

My daughter was born and she couldn't breathe because she had fluid in her lungs so they put her on a ventilator in the NICU and that same night she was born I found out my songwriting partner Adam was in a New York hospital with COVID-19 and was also on a ventilator which was just so on-the-nose and as his life and my daughter's life felt tethered together the concept of mortality suddenly hit me in a way it never had before and meanwhile the floor below the maternity ward was being turned into a COVID-only floor so everything was changing around us and furniture was being stored in the hallways and my doctor came to my room to check on me after birth and when she told us about maybe quarantining from her family to not infect them she burst into tears and then after we left the hospital my daughter was still in the NICU but my husband wasn't allowed back because of COVID regulations so he sanitized everything that had been in our hospital bags including microwaving some papers because who knows how the virus spreads and he did this as I went back and forth from the NICU and meanwhile I hadn't taken a shit in like five days but then we finally got to take our daughter home and Adam was getting better and I passed out in a blissful nap on the bed with the baby and the dog.

And then my husband woke me up to tell me that Adam died.

I spent the next few weeks dealing with so many contrasting

emotions at once that the word "intense" barely describes that time. There were moments in which I was breastfeeding my now-healthy daughter and feeling so grateful while at the same time weeping with grief for Adam. It's now June. My daughter is almost three months old and, although I feel more or less back to myself, my world is still upside-down. It still hasn't fully sunk in that one of the most important people in my life no longer exists. My daughter still hasn't been held by any of her grandparents. And any person that comes near us on the street might as well be radioactive because that's how quickly we get away from them. So as I immerse myself in editing a book about my relationship with the idea of "normal," suddenly that word doesn't represent some ethereal societal construct— it is, in hindsight, the entire world before March of 2020.

I could reinterpret the title of this book to now symbolize my longing for the normalcy of the past—that my urge to be where the normal people are means that I wish I could just go back in time and stay there. But I don't want to end on that note because, ugh, what a bummer and also my daughter wouldn't be there and I'm partial to her. So instead, let's say that wanting to live in normalcy is how I feel about the future. I long to skip over this moment in time and settle down in the new normal that's maybe even better and brighter than it was before. So let's say that's the new meaning of *I Want to Be Where the Normal People Are*.

Also, it's clear that the book title is a reference to *The Little Mermaid*, right?

Acknowledgments

I first want to acknowledge you for reading the acknowledgments. Whether you're sitting on the toilet passing the time, using this section as a way to teach your child to read, or just craved some more of my silky-smooth prose, thank you for being interested in the people I want to thank.

To organize my thoughts, I will be acknowledging everyone in the style of a Jewish girl inviting her friends and family to come up and light the candles at her Bat Mitzvah. I never had a Bat Mitzvah (I found that Hebrew school conflicted too much with theater), so, through this acknowledgment, I will finally be a woman under Jewish law.

To every assistant I had over the course of the three years it took me to get my shit together and write this book: Hailey Chavez, Ilana Peña, Ilana Wolpert, Elissa Aron, and Kelsey Flynn. A thank-you to Britney Young and Bola Ogun as well—they were my assistants before I got the book deal, but they helped keep me alive so that I could someday write this book.

I hope that getting me coffee was fun; come up and light candle number one.

To my editor, Suzanne O'Neill at Grand Central Publishing. Guys, an editor isn't just someone who looks through your book for typos and misplaced commas; they are basically the unofficial co-writer of any book.

Suzanne, you're the best unofficial co-writer anyone ever knew; come up and light candle number two.

To Aline Brosh McKenna for reading the entire book in less than a single day and then sending me detailed notes. I can't say I was surprised but I am no less grateful to her.

Aline, your kindness makes me go "whee!" Come up and light candle number three.

To Brendan for his insights on the theater chapter and for letting me use his real name in talking about our high school romance (but also letting me know when a certain detail was "too graphic").

I can't wait to be friends for eighty years more; Brendan, come up and light candle number four.

To my parents for assumedly respecting my wishes and not reading the erotica chapter.

For eighteen years you both kept me alive; come up and light candle number five.

To my literary representatives who guided me through this process; namely Richard Abate at 3 Arts and Brandi Bowles at UTA, as well as my lawyer Lev Ginsburg. Thanks also to Allan Haldeman, Josh Katz, Greg Walter, Josh Lieberman, Jeff Chassen, and Dominique Appel.

Let's all share a bowl of Kix; come up and light candle number six.

An acknowledgment of the composer and lyricist of the *Pepper Ann* theme song, Brian Woodbury, whose lyrics I excerpted in part one. Thank you, Brian, whose name is not Kevin; come up and light candle number seven.

Thank you to the marketing and publicity team at Grand Central Publishing: Jimmy Franco, Kamrun Nesa, Alli Rosenthal, Amanda Pritzker, and Andrew Duncan, as well as my personal publicists, Cara Tripicchio and Stephanie Kazanjian.

One time I saw the movie *Little Man Tate*; come up and light candle number eight.

To my dog, Wiley, who let me pick her brain in exchange for a belly rub.

You are too independent for me to refer to you as "mine"; come up and light candle number nine.

Thank you to Dan Gregor for so many things, but, most important, informing me that girls at Bat Mitzvahs light twelve candles, not thirteen, because the Torah says that women are responsible for their actions at twelve as opposed to men who are responsible for them at thirteen. Thank you for agreeing with me that this is fucked-up. And between your thorough notes on this book, your pandemic cooking, your unwavering support, and the fact you recently combined your genes with mine to make another person, you are, as always, the greatest partner anyone could ever ask for.

If I'm Anxious Barbie you're my Calming Ken; come up and light candle number ten.

To my daughter. I can't wait to get your thoughts on this book but also hope that you, too, skip the erotica chapter.

You are my pink pickle sent down from heaven; come and light candle number eleven.

And candle twelve is for a man who never calls a baseball cap a lid; to Jack Dolgen, who knows what he did.